RECENT MEASURES

I0149729

FOR THE

PROMOTION OF EDUCATION

IN

ENGLAND.

TENTH EDITION.

LONDON:

RIDGWAY, PICCADILLY.

MDCCCXXXIX.

A COPY of the REPORT of the COMMITTEE of COUNCIL appointed to superintend the Application of any Sums voted by Parliament for the purpose of promoting PUBLIC EDUCATION, of the 3d day of this instant June.

At the Court at Buckingham Palace, the 3d of June, 1839.

Present,

THE QUEEN'S MOST EXCELLENT MAJESTY IN COUNCIL.

WHEREAS there was this day read at the Board a Report from the Committee of Council appointed to superintend the application of any sums voted by Parliament for the purpose of promoting Public Education; which Report, dated the 1st of June, was in the words following; viz.

" Your Majesty having been pleased, by Your Order in Council of the 10th April 1839, to appoint us a Committee of Council to superintend the application of any Sums voted by Parliament for the purpose of promoting Public Education, we, the Lords of the said Committee, have this day met, and agreed humbly to present to Your Majesty the following Report :

" The Lords of the Committee recommend that the sum of Ten Thousand Pounds, granted by Parliament in 1835 towards the erection of Normal or Model Schools, be given in equal proportions to the National Society and the British and Foreign School Society. That the remainder of the subsequent Grants of the years 1837 and 1838, yet unappropriated, and any Grant that may be voted in the present year, be chiefly applied in aid of Subscriptions for building, and, in particular cases, for the support of Schools connected with those Societies; but that the rule hitherto adopted of making a Grant to those places where the largest proportion is subscribed be not invariably adhered to, should application be made from very poor and populous districts, where Subscriptions to a sufficient amount cannot be obtained.

" The Committee do not feel themselves precluded from

making Grants in particular cases, which shall appear to them to call for the aid of Government, although the applications may not come from either of the two mentioned Societies.

" The Committee are of opinion, that the most useful application of any sums voted by Parliament would consist in the employment of those monies in the establishment of a Normal School, under the direction of the State, and not placed under the management of a voluntary Society. The Committee, however, experience so much difficulty in reconciling conflicting views respecting the provisions which they are desirous to make in furtherance of Your Majesty's wish, that the children and teachers instructed in this School should be duly trained in the principles of the Christian religion, while the rights of conscience should be respected, that it is not in the power of the Committee to mature a plan for the accomplishment of this design without further consideration; and they therefore postpone taking any steps for this purpose until greater concurrence of opinion is found to prevail.

" The Committee recommend that no further Grant be made, now or hereafter, for the establishment or support of Normal Schools, or of any other Schools, unless the right of inspection be retained, in order to secure a conformity to the regulations and discipline established in the several Schools, with such improvements as may from time to time be suggested by the Committee.

" A part of any Grant voted in the present year may be usefully applied to the purposes of inspection, and to the means of acquiring a complete knowledge of the present state of Education in England and Wales."

Her Majesty, having taken the said Report into consideration, was pleased, by and with the advice of Her Privy Council, to approve thereof.

(Signed)   C. C. GREVILLE.

PREFACE.

In preceding editions of this pamphlet the following passage occurred immediately after the words " by constant superintendance," p. 55 :—" In the " House of Lords the Marquis of Lansdowne ob-" served, ' I said the State should provide for the " ' education; I did not say for the spiritual and " ' religious education, but for the secular education " ' of the people.' The Bishop of Exeter ' was glad " ' the Noble Marquis had given that explanation, " ' (hear, hear). He assented to the principle.' All " that remains, therefore, is, in providing for the " secular education of the people, to render the pro-" vision such that they shall not be excluded from " its benefits by religious tests. For this purpose it " may be necessary, in particular cases, to admit " some variation from the plans of the National So-" ciety and British and Foreign School Society. " Upon the principle thus elucidated by the discus-" sions in Parliament, we trust that all parties are " now agreed."

This passage, together with the words, " which has " been more fully illustrated in the debates," which occurred in page 55. after the words " one principle," are now omitted, in consequence of the correspondence between Lord John Russell and the Bishop of Exeter, published in these pages.

The passage quoted from the debate is confirmed by the report in the " *Times* " of July 6th, and in the " Mirror of Parliament," July 27th, with the exception of one word, " instruction " for " education."

But in the speech of the Bishop of Exeter subsequently published for circulation, as corrected by his Lordship, and which had not been examined until attention was drawn to it by the Right Reverend Prelate, the conversation assumes a different form. In the speech thus published, the conversation is thus reported : " *The Marquis of Lansdowne*—I said the " State should provide for the education of those who " dissent from the Church ; I did not say for their " spiritual and religious education, but for their " secular. *The Bishop of Exeter*—I rejoice to hear " this ; I rejoice to have given the Noble Marquis an " opportunity of making this important explanation ; " the more important, because it is explanation. My " Lords, the Noble Marquis disclaims the pernicious " principle, that the State may lawfully assist in

" teaching religious doctrines which it believes to be
" false."

This parliamentary conversation being now omitted
in the pages of this pamphlet, and the context brought
together without any other alteration than those stated
above, the sense in which the passage omitted was
understood, and the reason why it was quoted, may
be more apparent. We request the reader's attention
to the following exposition of what was intended to
be conveyed.

The Committee of Council proposed by their report
of the 3rd of June, to apportion the parliamentary
grant, chiefly—

1. In aid of Schools connected with the National
Society; in which, besides biblical instruction, the
doctrines of the Church of England are taught from
the catechism and formularies, and in which the
ritual of the Church is used.

2. In aid of Schools of the British and Foreign
School Society, in which religious instruction is confined to biblical reading.

3. To admit *certain exceptional cases* of Schools
not belonging either to the National Society, or to
the British and Foreign School Society.

The whole passage was intended to relate only to
these exceptional cases; and was quoted as elucidat-

ing the view supposed to be taken by the Marquis of Lansdowne and the Bishop of Exeter in relation to such exceptional cases.

The fact that the Committee of Council intended a large portion of the Parliamentary Grant to be appropriated to Schools in connection with the National Society, is evidence that the Committee recognised the paramount importance of providing for the direct inculcation of the doctrine, and use of the Ritual of the Established Church, as respects children of churchmen. The question under discussion in this particular passage, however, was not the duty of the State, to those within the pale of the Church, nor to the entire body of those without the pale of the Church, but to a fractional part of those without the pale of the Church.

Exeter, October 10, 1839.

My Lord,

On my return to Exeter, I have the honour of receiving your Lordship's letter of the 7th instant, and I thank you for the early answer which you have given to the questions I felt it my duty to propose.

I assent to your Lordship's suggestion, that this question would be more properly addressed to the President of the Council. But the notoriety of his absence from England made it necessary that I should address it to your Lordship, whose name stands in the list of the " Committee on Education" next to that of the Lord President.

Your Lordship having now informed me that you believe the Committee gave a general direction for the circulation of the pamphlet entitled " Recent Measures for the promotion of Education in England," and the cover of a copy of it now before me bearing on its margin a printed notice of its having been sent from the " Committee of Council on Education," as well as being superscribed " On Her Majesty's service," and sealed with the impress of " Privy Council," I cannot but regard the Committee as adopting, and therefore responsible for, the contents of the pamphlet. In consequence, I request your Lordship's attention to a most extraordinary misrepresentation made in it of words spoken by me in the House of Lords on the 5th of July last.

The passage to which I refer, is in pp. 55-6, and I quote it at length to prevent all misapprehension.

" One principle which has been more fully illustrated in the debates, is especially applicable to these cases, viz. that while the Government is most anxious that religious instruction should be united to secular, and will grant all proper facilities for that purpose, the State is peculiarly

b

charged with the duty of rendering secular instruction accessible to all, and with the improvement of the quality of such secular instruction by assistance from the public funds, and by constant superintendance. In the House of Lords the Marquis of Lansdowne observed, ' I said the state should provide for the education; I did not say for the spiritual and religious education, but for the secular education of the people.'—' The Bishop of Exeter was glad the Noble Marquis had given that explanation. He assented to the principle." Presently afterwards it is said, " Upon the principle thus elucidated by the discussion in Parliament, we trust that all parties are now agreed."

Now the plain and obvious import of this is, that in the discussion of the question in the House of Lords, I assented to the principle, that the duty of the state, in respect to the education of the people, is limited to " rendering secular instruction accessible to all," and to " the improvement of the quality of such secular instruction by assistance from the public funds, and by constant superintendance." But so far is this from being a correct statement, that it is contrary to the whole tenor of the speech delivered by me on that occasion. So manifest, indeed, is the perversion of my very plain meaning, that if it had occurred in an anonymous publication, I must have considered it as wilfully fraudulent. Bearing, however, as it does, the formal and official sanction of the " Committee on Education," I cannot ascribe it to any dishonourable motive; and I willingly impute it to some most strange, and utterly unaccountable misconception. That this is the gentlest description applicable to it, I proceed to satisfy your Lordship by citing a passage from the report of my speech, which I have the honour of enclosing, and which was corrected by myself, immediately after it had been delivered.

At pp. 5, 6, I was dealing with a question proposed to the Bench of Bishops by the Lord President—" Do they think

" that the Church has a right to the education of the people
" at large, including that portion of the people, millions in
" number, who do not belong to the Church ?" My answer
was as follows :—" The Church has no right to claim the en-
forcement of any system of education on the people, or any
part of the people, least of all on that part which does not
belong to the Church. But, my Lords, the Church has a
right to demand of the State—and if the State, as well as the
Church, is prepared to do it's duty, that demand will be
answered—the Church, I say, has a right to demand of the
State the means of *offering* education to all, whether they are
members of the Church, or not. God forbid that the Church
should have either the power, or the will, to compel any
persons, or class of persons, to accept its system of education!
But we have a right, my Lords, to demand, that the State,
acknowledging the Church to be the true Church, acknowledging it to profess and to teach the true Religion, and
thereby implying the duty of the Church to inculcate—aye,
and not only to inculcate, but to spread, that blessed truth
which it professes ; we have a right to demand that the State
shall supply the necessary means to enable the Church to
discharge its high functions. I ask, then, the Noble Marquis
to call on that Government, in which he bears so high a
place, to propose to Parliament such a grant, as will enable
the Church to educate all within its pale, who need public
aid ; and to offer to educate all without its pale, who will
accept the offer, in that holy religion which the Noble Marquis and his colleagues, and which the State itself, acknow-
ledge to be true ; and if true, of course to be alone true.
Will the Noble Marquis do this his duty ?"

I am not aware that I could have used words more directly
contrary to the sentiment ascribed to me in the Committee's
pamphlet, even if I had anticipated, and laboured to prevent,
the possibility of such a mis-statement.

At pp. 10, 11, of the enclosed, your Lordship will find the

interlocutory remarks between the Lord President and myself, which are more immediately referred to in the pamphlet; and on reading them you will observe, that they relate not to the point stated in the pamphlet, but to one of a very different kind, viz.—whether the State may assist in teaching religious doctrines, which it believes to be false.

Your Lordship will also perceive that I did not assent to the Lord President's principle; but the Lord President assented to mine, and joined me in disclaiming the pernicious principle, that the State may lawfully assist in teaching such doctrines. It is true that he qualified this disclaimer by limiting its operation to England; but this very limitation marks the more strongly the principle of which we were speaking, and which, as your Lordship perceives, is very different from that which is put into our mouths by the Committee's pamphlet.

I regret the absence of the Lord President; for he, I am confident, if he were in England, would confirm the accuracy of my statement; but I venture to refer your Lordship to any Noble Lord who attended to the debate.

Should your Lordship do me the honour of reading the whole of the reported speech, which I now enclose, you will not find a single sentence, which affords any shadow of justification of the passage of which I complain,—but very much which, if I mistake not, your Lordship will think directly contrary to it.

I have the honour to be,

My Lord,

Your Lordship's most obedient Servant,

H. EXETER.

The Right Honourable
The Lord John Russell, &c. &c.

Buckhurst, Oct. 15th, 1839.

My Lord,

I have had the honour of receiving your Lordship's letter of the 10th inst. It certainly appears to me that the writer of the pamphlet has mistaken your Lordship's meaning. He was probably misled by some incorrect report in the newspapers of what took place in the House of Lords. I will take care to suspend for the present any distribution of the pamphlet by the Committee of Privy Council.

I am much obliged to your Lordship for the copy of your Lordship's Speech delivered in the House of Lords upon the 5th of July of the present year—a speech marked by the ability which distinguishes all that proceeds from your Lordship. But I cannot but observe that there are some misconceptions of the design of the Members of the Committee quite as extraordinary as that which your Lordship has pointed out in the pamphlet. But I will not occupy your Lordship's time upon this subject, engaged as you now are in the labours of your diocese. I will therefore content myself with saying, that it has been the main object of the Committee to extend and encourage the religious instruction of the people, but that while they have endeavoured to insist on the instruction of the children of Churchmen in the doctrines of the Church of England, they have not conceived themselves justified in withholding all public aid for the instruction of those children of the poor whose parents conscientiously object to allow their children to be taught the Church Catechism, or to be compelled, as the price of their instruction, to attend divine service in any other than their own places of worship.

I have the honour, &c.

J. RUSSELL.

The Right Rev. the Lord Bishop of Exeter.

Exeter, 16th October, 1839.

My Lord,

I request your Lordship to accept my thanks for the letter of the 15th, which I have this day had the honour of receiving. The conclusion of that letter gives me peculiar gratification, as it shews that no practical difficulties need any longer to exist in combining due regard for the duties of the State to the Church, with full security to the rights of conscience in those who dissent from her doctrines, and do not join in her worship. For myself, I have no hesitation in avowing that, in my judgment, it would be wrong to " withhold all public aid for the instruction of those children of the poor, whose parents conscientiously object to allow their children to be taught the Church Catechism, or to be compelled, as the price of their instruction, to attend divine service in other than their own places of worship." I should rejoice to see instituted a conference between the " Committee of the Privy Council on Education" and the Bishops, for the purpose of devising measures to carry into effect your Lordship's very just and moderate principle, and at the same time to give to the Church that public recognition of her being the fit guardian and administratrix of National Education, with which your Lordship's principle can so well be reconciled.

The charge which I have delivered to my Clergy, and which has been announced for publication, has noticed the pamphlet sent forth by the Committee, entitled, " Recent Measures for the Promotion of Public Education in England," and has dealt with its contents as authorized by the Committee. Not only the passages read by me to my Clergy, but also a longer one prepared by me, in which I comment on that pamphlet, will make part of the Charge when published. In truth, your Lordship will perceive that the mere suspension of the circulation of a document which has already been dispersed so widely and so authoritatively will not remove the necessity of such comments, as I otherwise have thought it my duty to make.

It will give me, however, great pleasure to publish the correspondence which I have had the honour to hold with your Lordship, in my Appendix. It will, I am confident, be read, (especially that part of your Lordship's letter of the 15th, to which I have already referred) with the highest satisfaction by others, whose suffrages are more valuable than mine.

I have the honour to be,

My Lord,

Your Lordship's most obedient Servant,

H. EXETER.

The Right Hon.
The Lord John Russell,
    &c. &c. &c.

RECENT MEASURES,

&c. &c. &c.

CHAPTER I.

INTRODUCTION—STATE OF EDUCATION IN ENGLAND—EFFECTS ON CRIME—
REPORTS OF CHAPLAINS OF GAOLS—NECESSITY FOR INTERFERENCE OF
GOVERNMENT.

ALL plans which have been proposed for promoting National Education in England by calling into operation the powers of the Executive Government, have necessarily been subjected to the most searching scrutiny. The advocates of education must not however accept the earnestness with which public attention is directed to this subject as a measure of the degree in which the necessity of an extension and improvement of the elementary education of the poorer classes is recognized. It is indeed generally known that even the art of reading has been acquired by a portion only of the rising population, and by a smaller part of the adult working class; and that, as respects the rudimentary knowledge which might develope the understanding, and afford the labourer a clear view of his social position,—its duties, its difficulties, and rewards,—and thus enable him better to employ the powers with which Providence has gifted him, to promote his own comfort and the well-being of society, he is generally destitute, and what is worse, abandoned to the ill regulated and often pernicious agencies by which he is surrounded. It is commonly confessed that no sufficient means exist to train the habits of the children of our poorer classes,—to inspire them with healthful social and household sympathies,—with a love of domestic peace and social order,—with an enlightened reverence for revealed truth, and with the sentiment of piety and devotion.

But while these proofs of the fatal void in our national institutions are admitted, we fear we may not attribute the eagerness with which every proposal for the improvement and extension of popular education is discussed solely to an earnest and enlightened sympathy with the condition of the working classes. We must admit as a necessary element of our estimate of the popular feeling, the fact that the connection which exists in every well-devised plan for National Education between the secular and the religious instruction and moral training of the people, rouses the advocates of the antagonist principles involved in questions of civil and religious liberty, which have caused political struggles deeply affecting the middle and higher classes of society, but in the consequences of which the lower classes have hitherto had comparatively little practical interest.

The ferment occasioned by the recent settlement of some of these grave questions has not yet subsided, and to the state of public opinion, which has had its source in their prolonged discussion, we must attribute, in a great degree, the suspicion with which every proposal for the promotion of National Education is regarded, and the singular excitement produced by its announcement.

We are the last to deprecate public discussion—we invite it: we rejoice in the activity of the public mind—we have nothing to fear excepting from its apathy; our hopes are all concentrated in the right of private opinion—in the freedom with which, in this country, every question of public policy is debated, and in the consequent spread of a knowledge of the principles on which the changes demanded by the advance of civilization are based.

In the first movements of popular excitement, misrepresentation and clamour may mislead individuals or entire political or religious bodies into an opposition to plans, which on more attentive consideration they would have cordially approved. Nay, in any society in which the right of public discussion is admitted, it is the lot of every improvement to be misunderstood and misrepresented at its first announcement; the frame of society receives a shock at every change, even for the better, and in the first moments of surprise the entire community bestirs itself to ascertain whence comes the disturbance, and what is its object.

To enable every person interested in this national question to ascertain what is the plan of her Majesty's Government, and thus to prevent or to remove the consequences of industriously circulated misrepresentations;—to invite public discussion, and at the same time to provide it with a plain exposition of the principles and arrangements which we conceive to be involved in that plan, we have published the Report of the Committee of Council approved by her Majesty, with a few observations.

Evidence has been collected from time to time by Committees of the House of Commons, by voluntary societies, and by individuals, incontestably proving that the provision for the education of the poorer classes in England is most limited in extent and defective in quality. In the year 1816, the "Report from the Select Committee of the House of Commons on the Education of the Lower Orders in the Metropolis," of which Mr. Brougham was Chairman, states the Committee "have found reason to conclude that a very large number of poor children are wholly without the means of instruction, although their parents appear to be generally very desirous of obtaining that advantage for them." "They feel persuaded that the greatest advantages would result to this country from Parliament taking proper measures, in concurrence with the prevailing disposition of the community, for supplying the deficiency of the means of instruction which exists at present, and for extending the blessing to the poor of all descriptions."

In their Report in the year 1818, this Committee state " that a very great deficiency exists in the means of educating the poor wherever the population is thin and scattered over country districts. The efforts of individuals combined in societies are almost wholly confined to populous places."

On the 4th of May, 1835, Lord Brougham brought the subject of National Education before the House of Lords, by moving a series of resolutions, among which were the following :—

" 1. That although the number of schools, where some of the elementary branches of education are taught, are greatly increased within the last twenty years ; yet, that there exists a great deficiency of such schools, especially in the metropolis, and other great towns, and that the means of elementary education are peculiarly deficient in the counties of Middlesex and Lancaster.

" 2. That the kind of education given at the greater number of schools now established for the poorer classes of the people, is of a kind by no means sufficient for their instruction, being for the most part confined to reading, writing, and a little arithmetic ; whereas, at no greater expense, and in the same time, the children might easily be instructed in the elements of the more useful branches of knowledge, and thereby trained to sober, industrious, prudent and virtuous habits.

" 3. That the number of Infant Schools is exceedingly deficient and especially in those great towns, where they are most wanted, for improving the morals of the people, and preventing the commission of crimes.

" 4. That, while it is expedient to do nothing which may relax the efforts of private beneficence, in forming and supporting schools, or which may discourage the poorer classes of the people from contributing to the cost of educating their children, it is incumbent upon Parliament to aid in providing the effectual means of instruction, where these cannot be obtained, for the people.

" 5. That it is incumbent upon Parliament to encourage, in like manner, the establishment of Infant Schools, especially in the larger towns.

" 6. That, for the purpose of improving the kind of education given at schools for the people at large, it is expedient to establish, in several parts of the country, seminaries where good schoolmasters may be trained, and taught the duties of their profession."

The Committee on the Education of the poorer classes, over which Mr. Slaney presided in 1838, in their report say, " they apprehend that they have ample grounds for stating, throughout this vast metropolis, the means of useful daily instruction are lamentably deficient. It must be borne in mind, that in the various valuable reports made by the Statistical Societies of Manchester and London, and in much of the evidence adduced before your Committee, the worthless nature of the education supposed to be given in the common Day and Dame Schools, has been dwelt upon; so that in many places it may be left almost out of account."

" Your Committee now turn to the state of education in the large manufacturing, and sea-port towns, where the population has rapidly increased within the present century; they refer for particulars to the evidence taken before them, which appears to bear out the following results :—

" 1. That the kind of education given to the children of the working classes, is lamentably deficient.

" 2. That it extends (bad as it is), to but a small proportion of those who ought to receive it.

" 3. That without *some strenuous and persevering efforts be made on the part of the Government*, the greatest evils to all classes may follow from this neglect."

Place.	Population.	Children of Working Classes at Daily Schools, &c.		Total.
		Day and Dame Schools very indifferent.	Other better Schools.	
1836. Liverpool . . .	230,000	11,336	14,024	25,360*
1834. Manchester . . .	200,000	11,520	5,680	17,200*
1835.† Salford . . .	50,810	3,340	2,015	5,355*
—— Bury	20,000	1,648	803	2,451
1835 { Ashton . . Dukenfield . . Staley Bridge . }	47,800	. . . .	. . . .	2,496
1837. Birmingham . .	100,000	8,180	4,697	12,877‡
1837. Bristol . . .	112,438	4,135 Not including Private Schools.	1,119	5,254
1838. Brighton§ { B. and F. National. }	40,634 in 1831	{ 1,367 863	3,033 3,247	4,400 4,110
1838. Leeds . . B. & F.	123,393 in 1831	No return of Dame or Day, but only of Public Schools.	2,971	—
1838. ‖ Sheffield . . .	96,692 in 1831	3,359	5,905	9,264
Northamp- { B. and F. ton . { National.	20,000	{ 1,011 996	1,215 1,202	2,226 2,198
Reading . B. & F.	15,595 in 1831	297	962	1,259
Exeter . . .	28,242 in 1831	2,045	1,830 Including Evening.	3,875
1836.¶ York . . .	25,359 in 1831	1,494	2,697	4,191

The returns made to the Education Inquiry, undertaken in 1833 on the motion of Lord Kerry, were, from the great imperfec-

* Vide Reports of Statistical Society.
† Report of Manchester Statistical Society on a Manufacturing District, read at British Association. Ridgway, 1837.
‡ Vide Evidence, Riddall Wood.
§ Where " B. & F." or " National" are mentioned, it only means that the returns came through the Secretaries of those Societies.
‖ Report (B. & F.) excluding superior and middling Schools.
¶ Report of Statistical Society of Manchester, 1837.
  Note. The general result of all these Towns is that about one in twelve receive some sort of daily instruction, but only about one in twenty-four an education likely to be useful. In Leeds, only one in forty-one; in Birmingham, one in thirty-eight; in Manchester, one in thirty-five.

tion of our administrative machinery, exceedingly incorrect, as has been proved by the subsequent investigations of societies, and individuals. At the period of this inquiry, the population of England and Wales was 14,314,102; and the number of children between the ages of three and fifteen, estimated as bearing the same ratio to the population as in 1821, was 4,294,230; and the returns to the Education Inquiry give 1,276,947 children as in receipt of daily instruction. We must recur to the report of the Parliamentary Committee of 1838 for the quality of that instruction, which being for the most part conveyed in Dame, and common Day-schools, is to be regarded as almost worthless, if not, in many instances, pernicious. The number returned as attending Sunday Schools, in 1833, was 1,548,890, which is to be regarded as a cheering indication of the extent of the means at present in existence, for procuring an observance of the Sunday among the children of the labouring classes, and of conveying to them a limited amount of religious instruction upon that day, but cannot be accepted as an indication of the amount of the efficient means, for the intellectual development and moral and religious training, of the children of our working classes. The children between the ages of three and seven, estimated as bearing the same ratio to the population as in 1821, was 1,574,551; and all under this age must be regarded as fit only for Dame and Infant Schools.

But we have already remarked, that the returns to the Parliamentary Inquiry of 1833, are utterly insufficient to test the quality and extent of education in England and Wales; we must therefore have recourse to some of the laborious investigations, conducted impartially by Statistical Societies, into the extent of education provided for the poorer classes in certain districts.

In the Report of the Manchester Statistical Society, respecting the state of education in Manchester, Salford, Liverpool, Bury, and York, we find the population estimated as 533,000; and it has been calculated that the number of children of the working classes, from three to thirteen, for whom daily education should be provided, is 80,050; (one third having been deducted from the whole number of children between three and thirteen, for those privately educated, or employed, or sick, or prevented by casualties from attending school, and deducting the number attending superior private schools,) of these children 21,957 attend Endowed and Charity Schools, National and Lancasterian, and schools attached to public institutions, and Infant Schools.

Further, of the total number of 80,050 children who ought to be educated; 29,259 receive an almost worthless instruction, in Dame and common Day-schools, leaving 28,834 uneducated in any Week-day-schools. Therefore 58,093 *children, out of 80,050, either receive no weekly instruction, or instruction only in Dame or common Day-schools.*

The Reports of the Manchester Statistical Society shew the inefficiency of the instruction given in the Dame and common Day schools, which is confirmed by the Report of the Parliamentary Committee of 1838, which we have already quoted. In our Appendix, No. 1, we have given, in a tabular form, summaries of the results of these investigations.

Whenever inquiries of a similar character have been conducted in rural districts, they have exhibited an equally lamentable deficiency of the means of primary instruction, and as the physical agencies of civilization are in less active operation in rural districts than in towns, we fear that a large portion of our labouring population have already realized the description given by Adam Smith of the working classes of a nation whose instruction has been neglected by the Government.

What might be accomplished for the advancement of civilization, and for the eradication of crime by the introduction of a more efficient primary education of the working classes may in some slight degree be estimated from the following facts, showing the proportion of offenders to their respective intellectual conditions in the years 1836, 1837, and 1838.

	1836.	1837.	1838.
Wholly uninstructed, or having received only the first rudiments of learning .	85.85	87.93	87.81
Able to read and write well . . .	10.56	9.46	8.77
Instructed beyond reading and writing .	0.91	0.43	0,34
Intellectual condition not known .	2.68	2.18	2.08
	100	100	100

From this rule of moral inefficiency we fear we cannot exclude any class of schools as at present conducted, for the methods of teaching which at present prevail commit the instruction of the children even of our National and Lancasterian schools chiefly, if not solely, to the most proficient boys and girls ; and from these it is apparent that little or no *moral influence* capable of elevating the character of the scholars can proceed. The training of the habits and affections, and the adoption of systematic means to develope either the faculties or the feelings of the children, are therefore necessarily neglected. Such acquirements as are made in these schools result almost solely from an effort of the memory which receives a meagre supply of the most rudimentary knowledge, while in a great number, if not the majority of instances, as this knowledge is received with distaste, it is not retained long after the children leave the school, and besides exerting no influence on the character in after life is of little use in enabling its possessor even to improve his physical condition. But what is most lamentable, we may say most fearful, is the fact which Professor Pillans and Mr. Wood have fully exposed, that the religious instruction consists, chiefly if not solely, in committing to memory catechisms and formularies which are neither explained nor understood, and that thus not only are the great truths of Christianity not recommended to the rational capacity of the child, but the sympathies which they are calculated to rouse and to develope, and which form so essential a part of a lively faith and an operative sentiment of devotion are left uncultivated. While, however, we depict, with deep regret, the defects of the existing system of primary education, we render our hearty thanks to those individuals and societies, particularly the National and British and Foreign, which have taken even the first step in the intellectual advancement of the people; but we request them to contemplate with us with apprehension the facts disclosed in the following table, resulting from an examination respecting the education of 1,052 prisoners in the Penitentiary at Millbank.

EDUCATION OF PRISONERS IN THE PENITENTIARY.

		Total Number.	Of whom could not read.	Proportion of those who could not read to Total.
Schools connected with the Church.	National School . .	66	1	1 in 66
	Charity School, not on the National System	96	7	1 in 14
	Sunday School Church of England	96	18	1 in 5
Schools connected with Dissenters.	Sunday Schools, Dissenters	28	1	1 in 28
	Lancasterian, or Dissenting Schools . .	19	1	1 in 19
Common Day Schools		598	43	1 in 14
Attended no School of any kind		149		

SUMMARY.

Total Number educated in Schools connected with the Church .	258	of whom could not read 26, or 1 in 10
Total Number educated in Schools connected with Dissenters .	47	of whom could not read 2, or 1 in 23
Total Number educated in common Day Schools	598	of whom could not read 43, or 1 in 14
Total of the above . . .	903	of whom could not read 71, or 1 in 13
Number who attended no School of any kind	149	
	1052	

The results contained in the foregoing table are abundantly confirmed in all their details by the records of the prisons for juvenile offenders in this country.

Lord John Russell, in his Letter to the Lord President of the Council, says, " The reports of the chaplains of gaols show that to a large number of unfortunate prisoners a knowledge of the fundamental truths of natural and revealed religion has never been imparted."

The Report of the Chaplain respecting the prisoners of the county gaol at Bedford in 1838, states " that their great leading characteristic was ignorance, heathenish ignorance of the simplest truths." At Midsummer Quarter Session he reported that " as to the condition, mentally and morally, of his unhappy charge, he regretted to say it could scarcely be more ignorant or degraded. It was his conviction that no pen could depict in colours sufficiently dark the moral and spiritual ignorance and debasement of the vastly greater number of those unhappy beings who pass through the prisons." *

Respecting the county gaol of Hertford, the Visiting Magistrates report, " The schoolmaster has been regular and diligent in discharging the duties of his office. During the year there have been 72 discharged, exclusive of those who did not fall under his notice and instruction, of whom 30 had been taught to read the Psalms and New Testament imperfectly, or so far to improve themselves as to read well. Of the rest, some have progressed to a knowledge of most words of two syllables, and the remainder were totally ignorant, the short periods of their imprisonment not admitting of improvement."

The Report of the Chaplain of the House of Correction at Preston says, " The following table shows the amount of ignorance in the 1129 individuals committed for various offences during the year, and the connection subsisting between that and the causes which have led to their offences :—

DEGREES OF EDUCATION.	CAUSES OF CRIME.								
	Drinking.	Uncertain.	Idleness and BadCompany.	Temptation.	Want.	Confirmed Bad Habits.	Weak intellects.	Combination of Workmen.	Total.
1. Unable to read	139	215	49	5	59	72	7	8	554
2. Barely capable of reading	57	92	12	4	24	32	1		222
3. Can read the Testament	46	61	5	2	19	21		1	155
4. Can read fluently	14	14	1	1	3	4		1	38
5. Can read well, and write a little	71	50	6	3	17	5			152
6. Can read and write well	4	3		1			.		8
	331	435	73	16	122	134	8	10	1129

* Gaol returns under 4 Geo. 4, c. 64, and 5 Geo. 4, c. 12, dated 20th Feb. 1839.

" If we consider the educated criminals as represented by the amount of those who are able to ' read and write well,' the proportion is remarkably small: and the inference surely must be, that education prevents or restrains crime, either by the operation of those good and religious principles which it should be its great object to communicate; or, at the least, by giving a taste and capacity for pursuits incompatible with the low and debasing propensities which open the door to crime for the ignorant and sensual. On the other hand, it is evident that the greatest absolute amount of crime is the result of ignorance and drinking combined. It is also, I think, specially worthy of observation, that, as the scale of instruction rises, intoxication begins to exhibit itself as a gradually increasing cause of crime, until, with the educated, it appears paramount over every other which can be distinctly ascertained."

The following is an extract from the Report of the Chaplain of the County Gaol at Warwick, on the condition of the criminals confined in that prison, presented at the Michaelmas Sessions in 1836.

" Their condition as regards education, is this; of every twenty-four who are committed, on an average seven have been taught to read and write; eight can read only; and nine can do neither; most of those who can write can read tolerably well, though their writing is generally a very poor performance; but at least the half of those who can read only, do it very badly. With regard to those important parts of education, religion and morality, generally speaking, no instruction whatever appears to have been given to them; for in a vast majority of instances, the persons who come to prison are utterly ignorant both of the simplest truths of religion, and of the plainest precepts of morality. Further, it seldom happens that any effort has been made to bring the reasoning faculties into healthy exercise; and the mind being thus left blank, as far as regards every thing that is good, it ceases to be a wonder that evil principles should so readily be adopted. Indeed, where such a miserable system of education is found, as appears to prevail in many places, it were much better that nothing were attempted; for people often appear to learn only just sufficient to render ignorance conceited, and to supply them with fresh incentives to vice. As far as regards religious worship, it is very true that at some period of their lives most of the prisoners have attended a place of worship of some denomination, but very few have been taught to consider this as an imperative duty, but rather as a matter of indifference, which perhaps it may be better to do than leave undone."

Many similar extracts might be given from the reports of other chaplains of gaols, all confirmatory of the brutal state of ignorance exhibited by almost all the offenders who come under their observation; but these may suffice. We have, however, placed in the Appendix a table containing a summary of the proficiency of the prisoners in Norwich Castle in reading and writing at the time of their commitment, taken at different periods, from 1826 to 1835.*

But the consequences flowing from this neglect are not fully exhibited in such returns. The expense of the penal administration for the prevention, detection, and punishment of crime in England and Wales, amounts to £1,213,082,† and the number of juvenile offenders in the prisons last year was 12,000.

On the 12th of February, 1839, by her Majesty's command, Lord John Russell laid upon the table of the House of Commons the letter which he addressed by her Majesty's command to the President of the Council, with Lord Lansdowne's reply. His Lordship's letter commences with words which cannot be too attentively considered,—"My Lord, I have received her Majesty's command to make a communication to your Lordship on a subject of the greatest importance. Her Majesty has observed, with deep concern, the want of instruction which is still observable among the poorer classes of her subjects. All the inquiries which have been made show a deficiency in the general education of

* See Appendix, Table No. II.
† See Returns for 1834 and 1838.

the people, which is not in accordance with the character of a civilized and Christian nation."

In the Treatise on the Wealth of Nations, Adam Smith thus describes the condition of a people whose education is neglected by the Government :—

" In the progress of the division of labour, the employment of the far greater part of those who live by labour, that is, of the great body of the people comes to be confined to a few very simple operations, frequently to one or two. But the understandings of the greater part of men are necessarily formed by their ordinary employments. The man whose whole life is spent in performing a few simple operations, of which the effects too are perhaps always the same, or very nearly the same, has no occasion to exert his understanding, or to exercise his invention, in finding out expedients for removing difficulties which never occur. He naturally loses, therefore, the habit of exertion, and generally becomes as stupid and ignorant as is possible for a human creature to become. The torpor of his mind renders him not only incapable of relishing or bearing a part in any rational conversation, but of conceiving any generous, noble, or tender sentiment, and consequently of forming any just judgment concerning many even of the ordinary duties of private life. Of the great and extensive interests of his country he is altogether incapable of judging ; and unless very particular pains have been taken to render him otherwise, he is equally incapable of defending his country in war. The uniformity of his stationary life naturally corrupts the courage of his mind, and makes him regard with abhorrence the irregular, uncertain, and adventurous life of a soldier. It corrupts even the activity of his body, and renders him incapable of exerting his strength with vigour and perseverance in any other employment than that to which he has been bred. His dexterity at his own particular trade seems in this manner to be acquired at the expense of his intellectual, social, and martial virtues. But in every improved or civilised society, this is the state into which the labouring poor, that is, the great body of the people, must necessarily fall, unless Government takes some pains to prevent it."—B. v. c. i.

The calamity thus foreseen by our great economist is realised in the condition of our rural population. The abuses of the poor laws, together with the almost universal neglect of instruction, have reduced this class to a state of mental and physical torpor. The gradual absorption of our domestic manufactures in the great vortices of trade, left in the south-eastern counties of England a larger population on the soil than could be supported in comfort by agricultural labour only, yet the labourer reduced to the condition of a serf, was incapable of any independent exertions to procure employment by removing to the great seats of commerce, or embarking in some new sphere of enterprize like the more adventurous, because more intelligent Scottish population. Though the labouring class in these counties must often have suffered from continued want, few or none could be induced to emigrate—few or no recruits for the army could be procured—their struggles were confined to stupid contests with the overseer in which they suffered their wages to be swindled away.—Then when they found industry had no reward—that all were bound to toil, but had a right to be maintained like helots—acts of secret and sullen revenge ensued. They sought to extort by fear what they could no longer procure by virtuous exertion. Property seemed their enemy, therefore they wrapped in one indiscriminating flame the stacks and homesteads of the southern counties, seeking the improvement of their condition by the destruction of capital.

On the other hand, the rapid progress of our physical civilization has occasioned the growth of masses of manufacturing population, the instruction, and moral, and religious elevation of which have hitherto been neglected by the State. These communities exhibit alarming features ; labouring classes unmatched in the energy and hardihood with which they pursue their daily toil, yet thriftless, incapable of husbanding their means, or resisting sensual gratification : high wages and want under the same roof; while other portions of the same classes are struggling on the barest pittance with continual labour, abstinent by necessity. From opposite quarters misery and discontent are goading both. The Rev. Mr. Close, perpetual Curate of Cheltenham, says, in a sermon just published, " It is a well known fact, that in the manufacturing districts, where the highest wages are obtained, the greatest poverty often prevails; where money is easily acquired, it is as quickly spent, and often in feasting as well as drunkenness; persons in this rank of life will not unfrequently discover a degree of extravagance in the gratification of their appetites, which would astonish those who are much their superiors in station; expending a week's wages in one feast, heedless of the wants of their families to-morrow." At the next door to the high paid artisan, who has squandered his week's earnings on the Sunday's feast, pines the hand-loom weaver, exhausted with continual penury and toil.

Physical prosperity stimulates all the animal appetites, and if unaided by moral restraint wastes her resources, and instead of connecting content and peace with plenty, continually rouses the population to feverish exertion. Notwithstanding the high wages of the artisan, the wife commits her infant to a hireling, and leaves her domestic duties to work in the manufactory. The parents, to enable ill-regulated means to satisfy increasing wants, lead their children of a tender age to the same scene of continual exertion. Domestic virtue and household piety have little opportunity to thrive in a population alternating between protracted labour and repose, or too frequent sensual gratification. When all the animal powers are thus continually called into action, adversity is met with sullen discontent, or with fierce outbreaks of passionate disquiet. Whoever will promise less toil and more money, is a prophet in the manufacturing districts; and—in the absence of those who would teach, that comfort can only be secured by a cultivation of those domestic sympathies and household virtues, which spring from a well regulated mind, and prove that happiness depends upon those internal moral resources without which the greatest prosperity is often a curse,—prophets will always be found ready to teach the population to seek a remedy for the evils they endure by violent attempts at social change. To the ignorant man, who has only the sense of the continual necessity to labour, in order to gratify his unappeased desires for sensual gratification, and to meet the wants created by wasted means, who can be more welcome than he who comes with the golden promise of high wages and ease, instead of leading him to an enlightened estimate of his domestic and social duties, and teaching him how much a resolute will, under the influence of morality and religion, may do, even in adverse circumstances, to render the lot of the poor man peaceful and happy? Less work and more means have always therefore been the promises of every impostor who has practised on the ignorance, discontent, and suffering of the manufacturing population.

We shall have to speak, in subsequent pages, of the political and social combinations which have of late prevailed in the manufacturing districts; the Trades' Unions, in which incendiarism, personal violence, and even assassination, are practised for the unattainable object of sustaining the rate of wages above the level resulting from the natural laws of trade—and the more recent armed associations for political purposes, in which the working classes have been exhorted to obtain by force privileges withheld by the constitutional representatives of the people: results, which are all ascribable to the physical developement of the population having been more rapid than the growth of our intellectual, moral, and religious institutions.

On the other hand, it is cheering to know, that the accumulation of the people in masses renders them more accessible to the beneficial influence of well-regulated social institutions. Having once encountered the necessity of supplying the intellectual and moral wants of the labouring classes, knowledge and virtue will, with adequate agencies, make more rapid progress among a concentrated than a scattered population. So long as our artisans lived in cottages scattered over the moors of our northern, and the wolds of our southern counties, little danger might arise to the state from their universal ignorance, apathy, and want; but if the necessity for raising their moral and intellectual condition could, under such circumstances, have been as pressing as it now is, the difficulty of civilizing them would have been almost insuperable. In the concentrated population of our towns, the dangers arising from the neglect of the intellectual and moral culture of the working class are already imminent; and the consequences of permitting another generation to rise, without bending the powers of the executive government and of society to the great work of civilization and religion, for which the political and social events of every hour make a continual demand, must be social disquiet little short of revolution. But the same masses of population are equally open to all the beneficial influences derivable from a careful cultivation of their domestic and social habits; from the communication of knowledge enabling them to perceive their true relation to the other classes of society, and how dependent their interests are upon the stability of our institutions and the preservation of social order.

The law recognizes the duty devolving on property, as respects the education of the factory children, and we rejoice to believe that, under the guidance of men of high intelligence and benevolence, such as many of the most wealthy manufacturers are, we shall soon realize what are the fruits of a well-devised system of intellectual, moral, and religious training, in rendering the communities, in whose well being they have so deep a stake, examples of what may be effected by applying to the moral elevation of the population the same sagacity and perseverance which have occasioned its physical prosperity. A short time only will elapse before, in some of our great towns, the most influential inhabitants will combine for the erection and support of Model Schools. Such institutions will create and diffuse a more correct estimate of the value of Education, and will promote its spread.

For another neglected class also the State has interfered. Under the parochial system, the orphan, deserted, and illegitimate children—waifs of society—were scattered through the parochial workhouses of England, where they were promiscuously mingled with the idiots, the sick, the sturdy vagabond, and profligate women. From the parochial workhouses, the gaols and hulks recruited the ranks of crime. These children are now under the care of Boards of Guardians, separated from the adult paupers, and measures are in progress to educate them so as to render them efficient and virtuous members of society.

For the juvenile offenders the Government is carefully preparing a system of reformatory discipline and training, in which all the resources of the educator will be exhausted to redeem these outcasts from the depravity consequent on neglect and evil example.

Besides these signs of coming improvement, we hail, as a presage of no little importance, the fact that the subject of National Education has occupied the attention of the Houses of Parliament during five nights of anxious discussion. We never were so sanguine as to expect that the great embarrassments with which it is surrounded could be at once dispelled; but we have a confident belief that every hour increases the anxiety of all friends of our constitutional liberties and national institutions, to preserve both by the education of the people.

CHAPTER II.

Results of Reformation in European Protestant States— Scotland — Prussia — Confederation of the Rhine — Switzerland— Sweden — Norway— Denmark — Holland, &c. — Condition in Catholic States — Belgium — France—Comparative Resources in England.

One of the early consequences of the Reformation in Europe, with the exception of England, was the establishment of a system of elementary instruction. It was a natural consequence of the assertion of the right of private judgment, that every government should charge itself with the duty of raising the standard of knowledge among the mass of the people. Thus a century and a half has elapsed since the system of parochial education was established by an act of the Scottish Parliament, and we may now trace, in the industry, enterprize, and foresight of our Scottish fellow-subjects, and above all, in their household virtues and earnest patriotism—in their domestic piety and reverence for the public institutions and ceremonial of religion, the consequences of a system of National Education, which, whatever be its imperfections, (and they are numerous,) is, in many respects, adapted to the genius of their nation. Prussia, as early as 1736, declared the elementary education of the people to be an essential part of the policy of the state. In that year she provided for the erection and repair of school-houses by the communes; regulated the duties and privileges of the teachers; appropriated portions of the church revenues to the provision of their salaries; and provided from the public funds means to meet the contingent expenses of the schools. This law underwent successive improvements in the years 1763 and 1765. These edicts also provided for the inspection and due regulation of the schools; for the transmission of reports to the Government; for the examination of teachers by the school inspectors, and for the elevation of some of the principal schools of the newly acquired territory of Silesia to the character of Normal Schools. The preamble to the first of these statutes describes the condition of the elementary instruction of Prussia, in terms singularly appropriate to that of the primary education of England at this moment. The training of the rising population was extremely inefficient, on account of the incompetency of the teachers: in wide districts of the country the training of the children of the working class was almost utterly neglected. The spread of true religion—the maintenance of social order—the diffusion of useful knowledge and virtuous habits, and the cultivation of the industrial arts, could not be secured excepting by a system of education capable of raising the people from ignorance, and, in some districts, from semi-barbarism.*

* The late President of the United States, in his letters on Silesia, thus describes the Schools which Frederick the Great established in every village of Silesia. "At the time of the conquest of Silesia," says Mr. Adams, "education had seldom been made an object of the concern of governments; and Silesia, like the rest of Europe, was but wretchedly provided either with schools or teachers. In the small towns and villages, the schoolmasters were so poorly paid, that they could not subsist without practising some other trade besides their occupation as instructors; and they usually united the character of the Village Fiddler, with that of the Village Schoolmaster. Even of these, there were so few, that the children of the peasants in general, throughout the province, were left untaught. This was especially the case in Upper Silesia. Frederick issued an ordinance, that a school should be kept in every village, and that a competent subsistence should be provided for the schoolmaster, by the joint contributions of the lord of the village, and of the tenants, the superintendence of the schools was prescribed as the duty of the Clergy."

Mr. Adams then relates how Frederick carried into execution his great design, he describes the mission of Felbiger, to acquire a knowledge of the latest improvements in the art of teaching, and the consequent establishment of model schools at Breslau and Glatz, for the training of educators for the primary schools.

"After all these preparatory measures had been carried into effect," he says, "an ordinance was published in the year 1765, prescribing the mode of teaching as adopted in the seminaries, and the manner in which the Clergy should superintend the efficacious establishment of the system. The regulations of this ordinance prove the earnestness with which the King of Prussia laboured to spread the benefits of useful knowledge among his subjects. The teachers are directed to give plain instruction, and upon subjects applicable to the ordinary concerns of life; not merely to load the memory of their scholars with words, but to make things intelligible to their understanding; to habituate them to the use of their

We have not space to describe the consequences which followed the exertions of the Prussian Government, until the disastrous war of 1806 involved Prussia in embarrassments, which, for a time, impeded the progress of her social institutions. Nevertheless, even when she was subjected to the incursion of foreign armies, or to a foreign yoke, her Normal Schools had, between 1806 and 1816, increased from six to sixteen. A special department for the superintendence of public worship, public instruction, and medicine, was created by an ordinance issued on the peace of Tilsit in 1810, and successive ordinances have regulated the whole details of pub-

own reason, by explaining every object of the lesson, so that the children themselves may be able to explain it upon examination. The candidates for schoolkeeping must give specimens of their ability, by teaching at one of the schools connected with the seminary, in presence of the professors, that they may remark and correct any thing defective in the candidate's method. The school tax must be paid by the Lord and tenants, without distinction of religions. The boys must all be sent to school from their sixth to their thirteenth year, whether the parents are able to pay the school-tax or not, for the poor, the school money must be raised by collections. Every parent or guardian who neglects to send his child or pupil to school, without sufficient cause, is obliged to pay a double tax, for which the guardian shall have no allowance. Every curate must examine weekly, the children of the school in his parish. A general examination must be held annually by the deans of the districts of the schools within their respective precincts; and a report of the condition of the schools, the talents and attention of the schoolmasters, the state of the buildings, and the attendance of the children, made to the office of the Vicar-General, who is bound to transmit all these reports to the royal domain offices, from which orders are issued to supply the deficiencies in the schools. This system was at first prepared only for the Catholic schools; but it was afterwards adopted by most of the Lutheran consistories.

" The system had at first many difficulties to contend with. The indolence of the Catholic clergy was averse to the new and troublesome duty imposed upon them. Their zeal was alarmed at the danger arising from this diffusion of light to the stability of their Church; they considered alike the spirit of innovation, and the spirit of inquiry, as their natural enemies. But the firmness of the Government overcame every obstacle. There are now more than 3,500 schools established in the province. Before the seven years' war, there had not been more than one periodical journal or gazette published in the province at one time; while there are now no fewer than seventeen newspapers and magazines, which appear by the day, the week, the month, and the quarter, and many of them upon subjects generally useful, and which contain very valuable information on all the most interesting topics of discussion."

lic instruction, into the system of which we cannot now enter.

At the present moment, the extent of the existing provision for the education of the poorer classes, is remarkable. There are forty-five schools for the training of teachers in the several provinces, which are constantly educating 2583 teachers; but so vigilant is the Prussian Government, that the official reports state that a considerable number of the teachers still entrusted with the management of schools, have hitherto not obtained certificates of competency, and the annual supply of teachers is not adequate to the demand created by casualties, and the retirement of teachers from age and other causes. To the supply of these wants the attention of the Government is constantly directed.

In 1838, Prussia contained a population of 14,000,000; the number of public schools was 22,910, in which 27,575 teachers were employed, who educated 2,171,745 children (or one teacher to seventy-eight scholars); besides which, 117,982 children were educated at Middle and Burger schools. The number of children between five and fifteen, or of an age to go to school, was 2,830,328; the number of children receiving instruction in the schools was 2,289,727, so that only 540,601 children were not at school, in the whole body of children, between the ages of five and fifteen. The proportion of children at school to the population, being as one to six, it may be considered that the extent of the provision for education in Prussia, is complete as to quantity, though as regards quality, it is still susceptible of considerable improvement. In the great towns of Prussia, the proportion of children at school to the population was, in Berlin, one in ten; in Breslau, one in nine; in Cologne with Deuz, one in eight; in Konigsberg, one in nine; in Danzig, one in eleven; in Madgeburg, one in eight; in Elberfeld with Barmen, one in seven; in Aix-la-Chapelle, one in thirteen; in Posen, one in thirteen; in Stettin, one in ten. The interference with primary instruction in towns occasioned by the early employment of children in the manufactories, by the less settled habits of the population, and by other causes, is greater than in the country; and the proportion of one in eight, has been generally deemed a complete provision for the education of the poorer classes in towns. Though the number of children attending school in the principal cities of Prussia falls short of this proportion, it is greatly superior to the whole number attending school in the great towns of this country, even including the ill regulated common day and dame schools. The Prussian regulations respecting education are adapted to the character of the people, and in harmony with the general policy of the Government. The state of education in Prussia may be employed as a means of comparison between the extent and quality of the means of instruction existing in that country and our own, while we carefully bear in mind that any measures which may be adopted by the Government of this country may be required to differ as widely from the ordinances of Prussia as the character of the English people and the nature of the laws and institutions of this country differ from those of the Prussian nation.

The condition of education in some of the states of Germany is, perhaps, superior to that of any other portion of Europe. The developement of primary instruction in Saxe Weimar and Wurtemburg has, during the present century, been promoted by one of the greatest minds of modern times, which embodied the national characteristics of the genius of his countrymen so as to command their universal homage. We avail ourselves of a luminous account of the state of education in Germany, and its legitimate consequences, given in the Journal of Education,* by the learned and experienced traveller, Mr. Loudon, whose powers of observation and impartiality will command universal respect, and whose statements are so important as to deserve quotation, without abridgment. We have, therefore, placed them in a note.

* " The change for the better, consequent on the system of instruction introduced into ' Prussia,' seems to be inferior to that which has followed the introduction of National Schools into Wirtemburg, Baden, Bavaria, and generally in all those states included in what was formerly denominated, the Confederation of the Rhine. In Wirtemburg, indeed, the inhabitants have been pretty well supplied

The schools in the Protestant Cantons of Switzerland have long been under the direction of a Council of Education, appointed by the Government, and are frequented by one-sixth to

with the means of education for near a century past; but during the last thirty years, the system has been very greatly extended and improved. At present, not only in Wirtemburg, but also in Baden, Hesse, &c., a public school is established in every parish, and in some instances, in every hamlet. The Master receives, as in Scotland, a fixed salary from the parish, exclusive of a small fee from the pupils, varying according to their age, and the subjects in which they are instructed. The fees are fixed by Government, and are every where the same. Exclusive of the salaries and fees, the Masters are furnished with a house, a garden, and in most instances, a few acres of ground, corresponding to the glebes of the Scotch Clergy. The law requires that the children should be instructed in reading, writing, and arithmetic, and it is specially enacted that they shall be instructed in the principles of German grammar, and in composition. The books used in the schools of Wirtemburg, and Baden, and generally throughout Germany, are very superior to those used in similar establishments in this country. They consist of geographical, biographical, and historical works, and of elementary treatises on moral science, natural history, and the principles and practice of some of the most important and useful arts. In all the larger schools, the boys and girls are kept separate, and the latter, in addition to reading, writing, and arithmetic, are taught all sorts of needle-work, the knitting of stockings, the making of clothes, &c. receiving at the same time, lessons in the art of cookery, the management of children, &c. The supervision of the schools is intrusted, in every parish or commune, to a committee, consisting of a few of the principal inhabitants; the clergy of the parish, whether Protestants or Catholics, being always ex-officio members of the Committee. This body is entrusted with the duty of inspecting the school, and is bound to see that the Master does his duty, and that the children regularly attend. No particular system of religion is allowed to be taught in any of the schools of Wirtemburg, and most of the other Germanic States. The tuition of this important branch is left entirely to the Clergy, and the parents of the children, so that the sons and daughters of Catholics, Lutherans, Calvinists, Quakers, &c. frequent the same schools, and live in the most perfect harmony.

" In Bavaria, the beneficial consequences resulting from the establishment of a system of National Education have been more signal than in any other European country. Half a century ago, the Bavarians were the most ignorant, debauched, and slovenly people between the gulf of Genoa and the Baltic. (For proofs of what is now stated, see Riesbeck's Travels in Germany, Vol. I. cap. xi.) That they are at present patterns of morality, intelligence, and cleanliness, it would be going too far to affirm; but we are bold to say, that no people has ever made a more rapid advancement in the career of civilization, than they have made during the last thirty years. The late and present Kings of Bavaria, have been truly the fathers of their country; for they have not only swept away myriads of abuses, and one-tenth of the population. Considerable improvements have been introduced into the system of Swiss education during the last sixteen years. Berne, Geneva, Basle, and Argovia have been long distinguished by their zeal, and the Canton de

established a representative system of government, but they have laid the only sure foundations of permanent and real improvement, in the organization of a truly admirable system of National Education. A school has been established in every parish of Bavaria, to which, as already observed, every one is obliged to send his children, from the age of six to fourteen. Lyceums, Colleges, and Universities, have also been instituted for the use of those who are desirous of prosecuting their studies, and every facility is afforded for the acquisition of the best instruction at the lowest price. In Bavaria the schools are inspected, and reports regularly made upon their condition by properly qualified officers, appointed for that purpose by Government. There is a particular department in the Ministry of the Interior appropriated to the supervision of the different kinds of schools. We subjoin a list of the places of primary education, and the number of teachers, pupils, &c. in Bavaria in 1828.

Public or National Schools	-	5,394
Normal Schools	-	7

TEACHERS AND PUPILS.

Inspectors of Schools	-	286
Teachers	- -	7,114
Pupils of all classes, about		498,000

" Now, as the population of Bavaria is almost exactly four millions, it follows, that not less than one-eighth of the entire population is at school. This is a very high proportion, and shews conclusively how universally education is diffused. In Scotland, it is supposed that the individuals at school amount to about one-tenth of the entire population.

" Throughout Germany the greatest attention is paid, not merely to the acquirements of the Teachers, but also to their capacity for teaching. To ensure proficiency in this respect, normal or pattern schools have been established in all the principal towns, which are attended by those who are candidates for the situation of Master; who, besides being instructed in the branches they are to be employed in teaching, are at the same time instructed in the best methods of teaching, and in the conduct proper to be followed in the management of scholars. Some of these schools very justly enjoy a very high reputation; and their establishment has had the most powerful and salutary influence on the system of instruction. No one is admitted to the pattern schools under thirteen years of age, and candidates are obliged to have made considerable proficiency in various branches. At the famous Normal School of Rastadt, the pupils, among other indispensable requisites, are expected to be masters of the elements of music."—
See Quarterly Journal of Education, Vol. I. p. 29.

Vaud has recently made great exertions for the improvement of the methods pursued in its schools. Fribourg has been distinguished by the labours of Père Girard, whose schools in that town were the most successful development of the system of mutual instruction, which the Continent has yet witnessed. His method resembled, in some important respects, that pursued by Mr. Wood in the Edinburgh Sessional Schools. In the Protestant Cantons, the average number of pupils to each school is about 90, and the proportion to each teacher 70. No detailed accounts of the Normal Schools of Switzerland have reached this country, but we are informed by intelligent travellers that two Normal schools exist in the Canton of Berne; a very good one at Lausanne, in the Canton de Vaud; two in Argovia; a very large school at Küsnacht, near Zurich; one in Thurgovia, presided over by Vehrli, whose name is familiar to all who take an interest in the progress of education; two in St. Gall; a school in Appenzell, pronounced to be well conducted, and one at Schaffhausen, another in the Catholic Canton of Grisons, and a third in that of Lucerne. Besides these, there are doubtless others of which at present we have no account, and generally it may be stated, that the Protestant Cantons of Switzerland are nearly foremost in Europe, as respects primary education. Throughout these Cantons the superintendence of the schools by a Council of Education, appointed by the Government, and acting by means of Training Schools, and a system of active inspection, has been found not only efficient in promoting the progress of education, but in perfect harmony with the free constitutions of the Swiss Cantons.

In Sweden, Gustavus Vasa, in 1527, diffused the Lutheran doctrine over the whole country. This change in the religious institutions of the country harmonised with the wants and character of the people of that age. Though, however, the Swedish clergy are still in numbers equal to their task, and though their ecclesiastical discipline is admirable, the Church has ceased to be influenced by the genius of Protestantism. A spiritual tyranny represses the right of private judgment, and the people continue superstitious. In 1684, Charles XI. enacted that every one of his subjects should be able to read, that the curate should examine him in religion before he was admitted to the Holy Sacrament, and that nobody should be married who had not been confirmed. These enactments appear to account for the fact that the Swedish peasantry were, until towards the close of the last century, regarded as the most religious and best instructed working class in Europe. Before the present century, education in Sweden was almost solely parental; few children attended public schools, but in order to entitle them to the privileges of citizenship, they were instructed and trained by their parents at home. Since the latter part of the last century a rapid deterioration has taken place in Swedish manners and in the moral condition of the population. Mr. Laing traces this degeneration to the influence of a defective social system, in which some of the worst institutions of feudalism corrupt a people aroused from the incurious apathy of the middle ages. The system of parental instruction has been found insufficient to struggle against the demoralizing influence of misrule and imperfect laws, discouraging industry and merit, and impoverishing the mass—and the evil example of corrupt manners among the privileged classes. Of late years only has any attempt been made to provide a remedy for these formidable evils.

An elementary school for the training of teachers in the best methods has been established at Stockholm, and a committee for the revision of public education formed, by an order of the King in 1825, have reported their opinions on schools for the common people, on elementary schools, and on the universities. They recommend that a school be established in every parish for the children of the poorer class, where they may be instructed in reading, writing, arithmetic, religion, biblical history, church singing, linear drawing, history, geography, and gymnastic exercises. They also recommend that libraries of useful books be attached to each school. These measures have since the Report of the Committee, been in a state of progressive execution, and Sweden will soon enjoy institutions suited to the character of her people and the wants of the age.

A parochial system of primary instruction is established in Norway resembling that of Scotland, but partaking of the primitive character of the institutions of that country. The funds for the support of schools, are generally derived from endowments, from local taxes, subscriptions, &c. Manufacturers employing more than thirty workmen are obliged to provide schools for their children, and to pay the teachers. Several training schools for teachers exist, and it is the intention of the Government to extend and improve them. The population of Norway being thinly scattered over wide mountainous districts, the Government, besides the paid parochial teachers, has provided a class of itinerant teachers, who successively visit the hamlets of their districts, assembling and instructing the children in the usual elementary knowledge. In 1833, the population being about 1,000,000, Mr. Ewerloff stated the *fixed schools*, in Norway, to be 183, instructing 13,693 children of both sexes, and the number of ambulatory schools as 1610, instructing 132,632 children. Besides which there were in the vicinity of towns 55 regular schools, supported by the citizens, in which 600 or 700 children were instructed. (*Journal of Education.*)

In Denmark a general code of regulations for schools has existed since 1817, the condition of the primary instruction having previously to that period made satisfactory progress. The elementary schools of Denmark now amount to 4600, educating 278,500 children. The population is 2,000,000, and it is estimated that there are 300,000 children of an age to go to school. The entire population of Denmark may, therefore, be said to be receiving instruction.

Holland has long enjoyed the advantages of an advancing civilization. The institutions of the central states of Europe for the promotion of primary education procured at an early period in the Batavian Republic, spontaneous efforts from a sagacious people for the training and instruction of the poorer classes. The direct interference of the Government was reserved for the present century; and this is in no slight degree to be attributed to the labours of Pestalozzi in Switzerland, which called forth similar exertions from Van den Ende, from Prinsèn, and from Falk. Early in the present century the Normal School at Haarlem was established under the direction of Prinsèn. The superintendence of education was thrown upon the Minister of the Interior, assisted by the Inspector-General of Instruction. From this department a series of well-devised regulations have in successive years emanated, which have been gradually carried into execution by a system of inspection so devised as to be in perfect harmony with the municipal institutions of the country, and the character and feelings of the inhabitants. The Inspectors formed the medium of communication between the government, the municipal councils, the provincial authorities, and the committees and directors of schools. It is their duty to foster the exertions of the local communities, and to direct them to useful objects. The inspection of schools; the examination of teachers, and their special authorization, together with the diffusion of information concerning the best methods of teaching, the proper apparatus, and most useful books, are among the inspectors' duties. Every inspector visits the schools of his district at least twice every year; he has power to appoint local school commissions; but is himself under the authority of a commission of inspectors of each department, which assembles three times a year in the chief town of the province, to examine the reports of the local inspectors, and to discuss and settle all matters relating to the internal regulation of schools. Deputies from each departmental commission are sent to the council of inspectors at the Hague, which assembles annually to confer with the Inspector-General and the Minister of the Interior. Two normal schools now exist in Holland, in which a large body of teachers is trained; but it is a part of the discipline of the Dutch schools to select the most promising pupils, first, as assistants in the more mechanical arrangements of the school, and then to be trained successively in every department, and at the same time to receive such instruction, as may fit them, when they arrive at maturity, successfully to perform the duties of teachers in primary schools. Many of the pupils thus reared in the primary schools finish their education in the normal schools. Holland is now one of the best instructed countries in Europe; and the singular prudence, industry, moral habits, and religious feeling of the Dutch people are chiefly attributable to a system of education interwoven with the institutions and with the habits and feelings of the nation. Mr. Nicholls thus describes the connection between the religious and educational institutions of Holland. " As respects religion, the population of Holland is divided, in about equal proportions, into Catholic, Lutheran, and Protestants of the Reformed Calvinistic Church, and the ministers of each are supported by the state. The schools contain, without distinction, the children of every sect of Christians. The religious and moral instruction afforded to the children is taken from the pages of Holy Writ, and the whole course of education is mingled with a frequent reference to the great general evidences of revelation. Biblical history is taught, not as a dry narrative of facts, but as a storehouse of truths, calculated to influence the affections, to correct and elevate the manners, and to inspire sentiments of devotion and virtue. The great principles and truths of Christianity, in which all are agreed, are likewise carefully inculcated ; but those points which are the subjects of difference and religious controversy, form no part of the instructions of the schools. This department of religious teaching is confided to the ministers of each persuasion who discharge this portion of their duties out of the school : but within the schools the common ground of instruction is faithfully preserved, and they are consequently altogether free from the spirit of jealousy and proselytism. We witnessed the exercise of a class of the children of notables in Haarlem (according to the simultaneous method) respecting the death and resurrection of our Saviour, by a minister of the Lutheran Church. The class contained children of Catholics, Calvinists, and other denominations of Christians, as well as Lutherans; and all disputable doctrinal points were carefully avoided. The Lutherans are the smallest in number, the Calvinists the largest, and the Catholics about midway between the two; but all appear to live together in perfect amity, without the slightest distinction in the common intercourse of life; and this circumstance so extremely interesting in itself, no doubt facilitated the establishment of the general system of education here described, the effects of which are so apparent in the highly moral and intellectual condition of the Dutch people."

The proceedings of the States of Germany probably suggested to Frederick the great designs which he conceived for the moral, intellectual, and religious improvement of Silesia. From these States the influence of advancing civilization spread into Switzerland, Sweden, Denmark, and Holland. The wars which succeeded the French revolution kept back for a time the educational institutions of these states; yet even under a foreign yoke, and in the confusion consequent on rapid political changes, a gradual progress was made; every interval of quiet was, in Germany and Prussia, applied to the reparation of the consequences of foreign invasion, and the general peace was no sooner proclaimed than the Government of every Protestant state on the Continent sought to rescue the people from the demoralization consequent on a disorganizing war, and to prepare the means of future defence in the development of the moral force of her people. England alone appears in this respect to have misunderstood the genius of Protestantism. With the wealthiest and most enlightened aristocracy, the richest and most influential church, and the most enterprising middle class, her lower orders are, as a mass, more ignorant and less civilized than those of any other large Protestant country in Europe.

By reference to the following table, extracted from various authorities, it will be perceived how far we are correct in tracing to the Reformation the great impulse which education has given to the civilization of Europe.

Proportion of Scholars in Elementary Schools to whole Population.

	Pupil. Inhabitants
Thurgovia, Switzerland (1832) -	1 in 4·8
Zurich, Switzerland (1832) -	1 in 5
Argovia, Switzerland (1832) -	1 in 5·3
Bohemia (1833) - -	1 in 5·7
Wurtemburg - - -	1 in 6
Prussia (1838) - -	1 in 6
Baden (1830) - -	1 in 6
Drenthe, Province of, Holland (1835)	1 in 6
Saxony - - -	1 in 6
Province of Overyssel (1835) -	1 in 6·2
Canton of Neufchatel (1832) -	1 in 6·4
Frise (1833) - -	1 in 6·8
Norway (1834) - -	1 in 7
Denmark (1834) - -	1 in 7
Scotland (1834) - -	1 in 10·4
Bavaria (1831) - -	1 in 8
Austria (1832) - -	1 in 10
Belgium - - -	1 in 11·5
England - - -	1 in 11·5
Lombardy (1832) - -	1 in 12·6
France - - -	1 in 17·6
Ireland - - -	1 in 18
Roman States - -	1 in 50
Lucca - - -	1 in 53
Tuscany - - -	1 in 66
Portugal - - ·	1 in 88
Russia - - -	1 in 367

In England we have no normal schools deserving of the name; Scotland owes to spontaneous individual exertions the only model schools which exist in that country; and in Ireland, the Board of Education, obstructed by peculiar difficulties, is proceeding to complete the fabric of an institution for the training of teachers, as a part of the great mission of civilization with which it is entrusted in that distracted country. Meanwhile the Catholic states of Europe have caught the impulse communicated from Germany to the Protestant Governments. When Belgium was incorporated in the kingdom of the Netherlands, the present King of Holland planned and carried on for fourteen years, a series of measures for securing to the poorer classes an efficient education, which up to the Belgian revolution, were eminently successful. The entire proceedings of the Dutch Government, as related in the Reports of the Inspector-General of Education, are descriptive of the benefits derivable from a judicious and persevering application of the powers of the Executive to the improvement and extension of primary instruction, while the consequences of the law proclaiming the liberty of teaching, or in other words, abandoning primary education to the spontaneous agencies of society, are to be found in the almost complete ruin of all institutions for the primary education of the people in Belgium.

Since the year 1833, the Minister of the department of Public Instruction in France has been assiduously employed in the execution of the law of June, 1833, relating to primary instruction in that country. The translation of the reports of M. Cousin on the state of primary instruction in Prussia and in Holland, has made the English public universally acquainted with the inquiry which M. Cousin executed by direction of the French Government in those countries, on the results of which the French law of instruction was founded, and which has served as a guide to the department of public instruction in the execution of that law in France.

In the Report of M. Gillon, on the part of the Commission charged with the examination of the French budget of 1839, it is stated that there are seventy-six normal schools in France, training 2,500 teachers. No department now wants an establishment for the training of teachers; but ten are associated with others for the support of a common establishment, and many instructors throughout France are engaged in rearing educators from their most successful pupils.

The state of primary instruction at the end of the year 1837, was as follows :—

Communes without schools	-		5,663
Communes provided with schools	-		29,750
Boys' schools { Communal / Private		30,065 / 9,439 }	39,504
Girls' schools { Communal / Private		5,283 / 9,143 }	14,426
			53,930

The want of schools in some departments is still very great. The number of children attending school amounts to 2,654,492, whereas it is calculated from recent official returns of the population that the number of children between the age of five and twelve years, is upwards of 4,800,000; but one-fourth of the children in the schools are above twelve years of age ; the number of children therefore between five and twelve in actual attendance on the schools is 1,989,000; and on these premises it is calculated that there are

Boys {	At school	1,164,000 }	2,550,000
	Not attending school	1,386,000	
Girls {	At school	822,000 }	2,250,000
	Not attending school	1,428,000	

From these facts it appears that only five-twelfths of the whole number of children attend school.

The Report proceeds to deplore the fact that 2,811,000 children in France receive no other instruction than that which is given by their parents, the greater part of whom are the hardest worked and the most ignorant of the population. In 1830, however, the number of children of both sexes attending the primary schools was only 1,642,206, since which period an increase of 1,009,000 has occurred. In 1830 there were only 10,000 schools for girls; now there are 14,000. The Report continues:—Young people seldom instruct themselves when their infancy has been neglected. Of this, sufficient proof is given by the return made respecting those who are called by their age to partake in the operations of the military service.— A table has been prepared, in which they are classed according to the degree of instruction. From 1833 to 1836, the proportion of this class who could neither read nor write was nearly one-half. It should be remarked that this return relates to young men who should have been at school between the years 1825 and 1828, a period when primary instruction was encouraged in France more by the zeal of voluntary associations than by the intervention of the State. Now the whole influence of the Administration is applied to induce children to accept the instruction which is offered them, and it is evident that the number of the illiterate has diminished.

If, continues the Report, the influence of ignorance on crime were doubted, all uncertainty would be dispelled by the official table of the persons accused and convicted, just published by the Minister of Justice, for the administration of 1836, and which differs but little from previous returns.

		Men.	Women.	Total.
Accused;	neither able to read nor to write	3172	1067	4239
Ditto,	imperfectly instructed in reading and writing - - -	1853	220	2073
Ditto,	well instructed in reading & writing	620	45	665
Ditto,	having an instruction one degree superior - - -	248	7	255
		5893	1339	7232

France cannot be cited as a country exhibiting the effects of a well devised system of Education on the moral and religious condition of the people, because sufficient time has not yet been afforded for the success of the exertions of the French Government in the improvement and extension of the means of primary education in that country; neither can France be cited as an example that a high degree of secular instruction is found connected with a diminution of violence, but an increase of the crimes of fraud.

Mr. Porter has shewn that M. Guerry's conclusion respecting the diminution of the crimes of violence and the increase of the crimes of fraud in the direct ratio of the extent of primary instruction in France was drawn from one year only (1831), but was not found to be supported, as far as the extent of this increase of the crimes of fraud is concerned, by an examination of the same facts in a series of five years, including that selected by M. Guerry. The yearly average of 1829-30-31-32-33, was as follows in the four *most* instructed departments, and in the *four* least instructed, the population being nearly the same in the departments compared.

	Crimes against person.	Crimes against property.	Total No. of Criminals.	No. upon whom sentence of death, and of forced labour for life, and for terms of years, was passed.
Four most instructed Departments . . .	45	136	181	35
Four least instructed Departments . . .	60	132	198	41.6

See Trans. of Statistical Society of London, Vol. I. p. 97, folio edition.

This result reduces the annual average excess of offenders against property in the four most instructed departments to 4 in 132, or about three per cent. We have before shewn that France cannot be regarded as a country enjoying the benefits of a well devised system of primary instruction, either as respects the extent or quality of the existing means of education, and we are inclined to agree with the following remarks of Mr. Porter on these facts as applicable to a country in that stage of civilization :—" Crimes against property may be considered as among the consequences of civilization, since it is evident

that the temptation to commit them must be greatest when the
artificial wants of man are the most numerous and urgent, and
where the accumulation of the means for their gratification is
most considerable."

We have already shewn that nearly all the crime in France is
committed by persons who are ignorant, and, within a fraction,
all the crime is confined to those whose instruction has been
limited to reading and writing merely. Mr. Porter proves that
this was equally true in the year selected by M. Guerry, and
that therefore the excess of crimes against property in the four
most instructed departments in that year is *attributable solely
to the physical influences of civilization on the uninstructed
part of the population.* If we separate the criminals of the
eight departments under examination according to this classification, we shall find that, in the year 1831, they were divided
as follow :—

	Four *most* Instructed Departments.	Four *least* Instructed Departments.
Class 1. Those wholly uninstructed - - -	101	158
2. Those who read and write imperfectly - - - - - - -	103	12
3. Those who read and write well -	24	13
4. Those still further educated - -	4	4
	232	187

The deductions of M. Guerry are thus entirely disproved from
his own data, a result which it is to be regretted should have
been overlooked in some recent discussions.*

* The following extract from Mr. Porter's paper contains facts too important
to be omitted, though, perhaps, too elaborate for the text.

" We have seen that in the more enlightened departments the proportion of persons who can read and write is 73 in 100, while in the least instructed it is no
more than 13 in 100. The population of the first being 1,142,454, it follows that
only 308,463 persons are wholly uninstructed; and the number of offenders in this
class being 101, it further follows that one person in 3,054 among them has been

The influence of instruction superior to that of mere reading and writing may be estimated also from the subjoined table from which " it will be seen that out of 50 persons sentenced to death, not one belonged to the well educated class; that 47 in that class were subjected to only slight correctional punishments, and four to simple surveillance; leaving only 49 well educated persons out of the whole population of more than 32 millions, or 1 in 664,678 persons, who, in the course of the year 1833 were considered deserving of punishments in any degree severe."

Punishments.	Cannot read or write.	Read and write imperfectly.	Read and write well.	Superior degree of instruction.	Total.
Death . . .	34	10	6	..	50
Perpetual Labour . .	90	44	4	3	141
Labour for different periods	483	235	67	17	802
Solitary Confinement .	437	213	64	23	737
Transportation . .	1	..	..	3	4
Imprisonment . .	13	4	1	3	21
Correctional Punishments .	1544	628	198	47	2417
Children detained . .	16	7	2	..	25
Surveillance . .	10	8	3	4	25
	2,628	1,149	345	100	4,222
	3,777 89.4 per cent.		8.2 per cent.	2.4 per cent.	100 per cent.

Results exactly similar are contained in the returns for 1834,

brought before the tribunals; whereas, among the three instructed classes the offenders are 131 among 833,991 instructed persons, or only one in 6,366.

" In the least instructed departments a similar examination gives us the following result;—the population being 1,134,280, of whom only 13 in 100 are instructed, there will be 986,824 wholly ignorant, and 147,456 who can read or write. The number of wholly ignorant offenders being 158, gives in that class only one offender in 6,245 persons; whereas the instructed classes, amounting in number to 147, 456, include 29 offenders, or one in every 5,084 individuals.

" It is not difficult to account for these results. In situations where education is pretty generally imparted, the wholly ignorant will find themselves at a disadvantage, through the greater portion of employments being occupied by those who are instructed. The ignorant man is therefore more impelled to lawless courses than in other situations, where the great bulk of the people being equally uninstructed, all have a nearly equal chance of obtaining honest employment."

1835, and 1836, which it would, however, be superfluous to insert.

But if this be the state of primary education in the Continental states, what, we are entitled to ask, ought to be its condition in England? Our political atmosphere has been comparatively serene; our social institutions have not suffered the shock of any disastrous revolution; our country has not been ravaged, as has been the fate of every Continental state, by any armies. The great territorial possessions of our aristocracy, are but so many stores of wealth and power, by which the civilization of the people might be promoted. In every English proprietor's domain there ought to be, as in many there are, Schoolhouses with well trained masters, competent and zealous to rear the population in obedience to the laws, in submission to their superiors, and to fit them to strengthen the institutions of their country by their domestic virtues, their sobriety, their industry, and forethought, by the steadiness of purpose with which they pursue their daily labour, by the enterprise with which they recover from calamity, and by the strength of heart with which they are prepared to grapple with the enemies of their country. How striking is the contrast which the estates of the landed proprietors of almost all other European countries bear in all that relates to material wealth, to the domains of our English aristocracy! On the Continent you are met on every side by the proofs of meagre or exhausted resources. In England we have no excuse; we have proofs of how much can be effected and at how little cost by the well directed energy of individuals, and we have in our eye examples among our peerage which cannot but be imitated as soon as they are generally known and appreciated.

Our great commercial cities and manufacturing towns contain middle classes whose wealth, enterprise, and intelligence have no successful rivals in Europe; they have made this country the mart of the whole earth; they have covered the seas with their ships, exploring every inlet, estuary or river which affords them a chance of successful trade. They have colonized almost every accessible region, and from all these sources, as well as from the nightly and daily toil of our working classes in mines, in manufactories, and workshops, in every form of hardy and continued exertion on the sea and on the shore, wealth has been derived, which has supported England in unexampled struggles ; yet between the merchants and manufacturers of this country and the poorer class there is little or no alliance, excepting that of mutual interest. But the critical events of this very hour are full of warning, that the ignorance, nay the barbarism, of large portions of our fellow-countrymen, can no longer be neglected, if we are not prepared to substitute a military tyranny or anarchy for the moral subjection which has hitherto been the only safeguard of England. At this hour military force alone retains in sub-jection great masses of the operative population, beneath whose outrages, if not thus restrained, the wealth and institutions of society would fall. The manufacturers and merchants of England must know what interest they have in the civilization of the working population, and ere this we trust they are conscious not merely how deep is their stake in the moral, intellectual, and religious advancement of the labouring class, but how deep is their responsibility to employ for this end the vast resources at their command.

In one other respect England stands in the strongest contrast with the Continental states as to the extent of her means for educational improvement. It is scarcely credible that with primary education in utter ruin we should possess educational endowments to the extent of half a million annually, which are either, to a large extent, misapplied, or are used for the support of such feeble and inefficient methods of instruction as to render little service to the community. Whenever the Government shall bend its efforts to combine, for the national advantage, all these great resources, we have no fears for our country. We perceive in it energies possessed by no other nation—partly attributable to the genius of our race ; to a large extent derived from the spirit of our policy, which has admitted constant progression in our social institutions; in no small degree to our insular situation, which makes the sea at once the guardian of our liberties and the source of our wealth. But any further delay in the adoption of energetic measures for the elementary education of her working classes is fraught, both with intestine and foreign danger—no one can stay the physical influences of wealth—some knowledge the people will acquire by the mere intercourse of society—many appetites are stimulated by a mere physical advancement. With increasing wants comes an increase of discontent, among a people who have only knowledge enough to make them eager for additional enjoyments, and have never yet been sufficiently educated to frame rational wishes and to pursue them by rational means. The mere physical influences of civilization will not, we fear, make them more moral or religious, better subjects of the state, or better Christians, unless to these be superadded the benefits of an education calculated to develop the entire moral and intellectual capacity of the whole population.

A great change has taken place in the moral and intellectual state of the working classes during the last half century. Formerly, they considered their poverty and sufferings as inevitable, as far as they thought about their origin at all; now, rightly or wrongly, they attribute their sufferings to political causes; they think that by a change in political institutions their condition can be enormously ameliorated. The great Chartist petition recently presented by Mr. Attwood, affords ample evidence of the prevalence of the restless desire for organic changes, and for violent political measures, which pervades the manufacturing districts, and which is every day increasing. This agitation is no recent matter; it has assumed various other forms in the last thirty years, in all of which the manufacturing population have shown how readily masses of ignorance, discontent, and suffering, may be misled. At no period within our memory, have the manufacturing districts been free from some form of agitation for unattainable objects referable to these causes. At one period, Luddism prevailed; at another, machine-breaking ; at successive periods the Trades' Unions have endeavoured in strikes, by hired bands of ruffians, and by assassination, to sustain the rate of wages above that determined by the natural laws of trade ; panics have been excited among the working classes, and severe runs upon the savings' banks effected from time to time. At one time they have been taught to believe that they could obtain the same wages if an eight hours' bill were passed, as if the law permitted them to labour twelve hours in the day ; and mills were actually worked on this principle for some weeks, to rivet the conviction in the minds of the working class. The agitation becomes constantly more systematic and better organized, because there is a greater demand for it among the masses, and it is more profitable to the leaders. It is vain to hope that this spirit will subside spontaneously, or that it can be suppressed by coercion. Chartism, an armed political monster, has at length sprung from the soil on which the struggle for the forcible repression of these evils has occurred. It is as certain as any thing future is certain, that the anarchical spirit of the Chartist association will, if left to the operation of the causes now in activity, become every year more formidable. The Chartists think that it is in the power of Government to raise the rate of wages by interfering between the employer and the workman ; they imagine that this can be accomplished by a maximum of prices and minimum of wages, or some similar contrivance ; and a considerable portion of them believe that the burden of taxation and of all " fixed charges," (to use Mr. Attwood's expression,) ought to be reduced by issuing inconvertible paper, and thus depreciating the currency. They are confident that a Parliament, chosen by universal suffrage, would be so completely under the dominion of the working classes, as to carry these measures into effect ; and therefore they petition for universal suffrage, treating all truly remedial measures as unworthy of their notice, or as obstacles to the attainment of the only objects really important. Now the sole effectual means of preventing the tremendous evils with which the anarchical spirit of the manufacturing population threatens the country, is by giving the working people a good secular education, to enable them to understand the true causes which determine their physical condition, and regulate the distribution of wealth among the several classes of society. Sufficient intelligence and information to appreciate these causes might be diffused by an education which could easily be brought within the reach of the entire population, though it would necessarily comprehend more than the mere rudiments of instrumental knowledge.

We are far from being alarmists; we write neither under the influence of undue fear, nor with a wish to inspire undue fear into others. The opinions which we have expressed are founded on a careful observation of the proceedings and speeches of the Chartists, and of their predecessors in agitation in the manufacturing districts for many years, as reported in their newspapers; and have been as deliberately formed as they are deliberately expressed. We confess that we cannot contemplate with unconcern the vast physical force which is now moved by men so ignorant and so unprincipled as the Chartist leaders; and without expecting such internal convulsions as may deserve the name of *civil war*, we think it highly probable that persons and property will, in certain parts of the country, be so exposed to violence, as materially to affect the prosperity of our manufactures and commerce; to shake the mutual confidence of mercantile men, and to diminish the stability of our political and social institutions. That the country will ultimately recover from these internal convulsions we think, judging from its past history, highly probable; but the recovery will be effected by the painful process of teaching the working classes, by actual experience, that the violent measures which they desire do not tend to improve their condition.

It is astonishing to us, that the party calling themselves Conservative, should not lead the van in promoting the diffusion of that knowledge among the working classes, which tends beyond any thing else to promote the security of property and the maintenance of public order. To restore the working classes to their former state of incurious and contented apatny is impossible, if it were desirable. If they are to have knowledge, surely it is the part of a wise and virtuous Government to do all in its power to secure to them useful knowledge, and to guard them against pernicious opinions.

We have already said that all instruction should be hallowed by the influence of religion; but we hold it to be equally absurd and short-sighted to withhold secular instruction, on the ground that religion is alone sufficient.

We do not, however, advocate that form of religious instruction which merely loads the memory, without developing the understanding, or which fails to stir the sympathies of our nature to their inmost springs. There is a form of instruction in religion which leaves the recipient at the mercy of any religious or political fanatic, who may dare to use the sacred pages as texts in support of imposture. We have seen that even a maniac may lead the people to worship him as the Messiah, whose second coming, spoken of in the pages of Holy Writ, was fulfilled. Many of the Chartists proclaim themselves Missionaries of Christianity. They know how to rouse the superstition of an ignorant population in favour of their doctrines, by employing passages of Scripture, the true meaning of which the uninstructed mass do not reach. They continually set before them those verses which speak of the rich man as an oppressor —which shew with how much difficulty the rich shall enter the kingdom of heaven. Poverty is the Lazarus, whom they place in Abraham's bosom—wealth the Dives, whom they doom to hell. They find passages in the writings of the Apostles speaking of a community of goods among the early Christians ; on this they found the doctrines of the Socialists. Our Saviour, in the synagogue of Nazareth, opened the Scripture at the prophecy in which Isaiah describes His divine mission: " The Spirit of the Lord is upon me, because he hath anointed me to preach the gospel to the poor, &c." From these and similar passages, they gather the sanctions of their own mission. Christianity, in their hands, becomes the most frantic democracy, and democracy is clothed with the sanctions of religion. Even the arming of the Chartist association is derived from our Saviour's injunction, " he that hath no sword, let him sell his garment and buy one." To such purposes may the Scriptures be wrested by unscrupulous men who have practised on the ignorance, discontent, and suffering of the mass.

Their power will continue as long as the people are without sufficient intelligence to discern in what the fearful error of such impiety consists. There are times in which it is necessary that every man should be prepared to give a reason for the faith that is in him. We loathe a merely speculative religion, which does not purify the motives; and which robs piety alike of humility and charity; but when the teachers of the great mass of the people unite the imposture of religious and political fanatics, preaching antisocial doctrines, as though they were a gospel of truth, the knowledge of the people must be increased, and their intellectual powers strengthened, so as to enable them to grapple with the error and to overcome it.

Next to the prevalence of true religion, we most earnestly desire that the people should know how their interests are inseparable from those of the other orders of society; and we will not stop to demonstrate so obvious a truth as that secular knowledge, easily accessible, but most powerful in its influence, is necessary to this end.

If, on the other hand, an opponent of popular education should admit the existence of the evil and the sufficiency of the remedy, but should refuse to apply it because it would violate his notions of the duty of the Government to diffuse the orthodox faith, we can only say that such a person is unfit for the government of men in the nineteenth century, and that he is sacrificing to his own opinions upon abstruse questions of theology, the certain and demonstrable temporal happiness of millions of his fellow-creatures.

CHAPTER III.

RECENT PROCEEDINGS OF HER MAJESTY'S GOVERNMENT — LORD JOHN RUSSELL'S LETTER TO THE LORD PRESIDENT OF THE COUNCIL — MINUTE OF THE COMMITTEE OF COUNCIL OF THE THIRD OF JUNE.

SINCE the reform of the Representation, the state of education in England, has, during three sessions, occupied the attention of Committees of the House of Commons. It has also incidentally been brought under the notice of various Commissions of Inquiry and departments of administration; but the Government has not yet proposed to Parliament any general plan for the improvement and extension of primary education. The difficulty of devising a system consistent with the principles of civil and religious liberty, and at the same time capable of combining all parties, and all religious denominations, has hitherto appeared to be insurmountable. The Government has therefore confined its interference to preliminary and experimental measures, which only indicate the embarrassment with which this question is surrounded, and its desire to surmount them.

Lord Althorp procured the consent of the House of Commons to a vote of £20,000., for the building of School houses in England and Wales, which has since been annually voted, as well as the sum of £10,000. for similar purposes in Scotland. The appropriation of these grants was confided to the Treasury, by which, in England and Wales, they were distributed, through the medium of the National Society, and of the British and Foreign School Society,* On the 30th of August, 1833, the Chancellor

* *Copy of Treasury Minute, dated 30th August, 1833.*

My Lords read the Act of the last Session, by which a sum of £20,000. is granted to His Majesty to be issued in aid of private subscriptions for the erection of Schools for the Education of the Children of the poorer classes in Great Britain.

The Chancellor of the Exchequer feeling it absolutely necessary that certain fixed Rules should be laid down by the Treasury, for their guidance in this matter, of the Exchequer proposed the rules contained in the subjoined note, to regulate the distribution of the sums annually voted by the House of Commons. Respecting the proceedings of the Treasury on these rules, the Archbishop of Canterbury, in the recent debate in the House of Lords, said, " he would appeal to the consciences of the Clergy in general, whether with respect to the grant of £20,000, which of late years had been given by the Government, very laudably and liberally, to the schools connected with the National School Society, and the Lancasterian School Society, they had ever complained of the share which the Dissenters in the Lancasterian Schools had had in that grant. They took the share belonging them, not only without complaint, but with thankfulness, and never inquired into the proportion in which it was distributed. They were satisfied with the grant, considering it as a temporary expedient. Lord Althorp said,

so as to render this sum most generally useful for the purposes contemplated by the grant, submits the following arrangements for the consideration of the Board.

1st. That no portion of this sum be applied to any purpose whatever, except for the erection of New School Houses, and that in the definition of a School House, the residence for Masters or Attendants be not included.

2nd. That no application be entertained unless a sum be raised by private contribution, equal at the least to one-half of the total estimated expenditure.

3rd. That the amount of private subscription be received, expended, and accounted for, before any issue of public money for such School be directed.

4th. That no application be complied with, unless upon the consideration of such a Report, either from the National School Society, or the British and Foreign School Society, as shall satisfy this Board that the case is one deserving of attention, and there is a reasonable expectation that the School may be permanently supported.

5th. That the applicants whose cases are favourably entertained, be required to bind themselves to submit to any audit of their accounts which this Board may direct, as well as to such periodical Reports respecting the state of their Schools, and the number of scholars educated, as may be called for.

6th. That in considering the applications made to the Board, a preference be given to such applications as come from large Cities and Towns, in which the necessity of assisting in the erection of Schools is most pressing, and that due inquiries should also be made before any such application be acceded to, whether there may not be charitable funds, or public and private endowments, that might render any further grants inexpedient or unnecessary.

In these Suggestions My Lords concur.

when he brought forward the resolution, that he proposed it only as an experiment. It was an experiment, however, which had succeeded extremely well, and the money, as far as it went, had been most usefully expended. They considered it then as an experiment,—as a temporary expedient—and no better could have been imagined as such ; but, at the same time, they looked forward to the period when a permanent system would be established by Parliament,—when a plan of education would be definitively settled. They conceived that the whole matter would be referred to the consideration of the legislature, and that the liberality of Parliament would be, as it had been, distributed equally to all who might be entitled to it."

The exertions of the National, and British and Foreign School Societies, in connexion with the assistance thus granted, are thus acknowledged in Lord John Russell's letter to the Lord President. " It is some consolation to her Majesty to perceive that, of late years, the zeal for popular education has increased ; that the Established Church has made great efforts to promote the building of schools, and that the National, and British and Foreign School Societies, have actively endeavoured to stimulate the liberality of the benevolent and enlightened friends of general education.

" Still," his Lordship continues, " much remains to be done ; and among the chief defects yet subsisting, may be reckoned the insufficient number of qualified Schoolmasters—the imperfect method of teaching which prevails in, perhaps, the greater number of the schools—the absence of any sufficient inspection of the schools, and examination of the nature of the instruction given—the want of a Model School, which might serve for the example of those Societies and Committees, which anxiously seek to improve their own methods of teaching ; and finally, the neglect of this great subject among the enactments of our voluminous legislation.

" Some of these defects appear to admit of an immediate remedy, and I am directed by Her Majesty to desire, in the first place, that your Lordship, with four other of the Queen's servants, should form a Board, or Committee, for the consideration of all matters affecting the Education of the People.

" For the present it is thought advisable that this Board should consist of

The Lord President of the Council.

The Lord Privy Seal.

The Chancellor of the Exchequer.

The Secretary of State for the Home Department, and

The Master of the Mint.

" It is proposed that the Board should be entrusted with the application of any sums which may be voted by Parliament, for the purposes of Education in England and Wales."

A Committee of Council on Education was accordingly appointed on the 10th April, 1839—and it should be observed that the functions of the Committee are limited to " superintend the application of any sums voted by Parliament for the purpose of promoting public Education :" These functions are therefore precisely similar to those which were exercised by the Treasury in the years 1835, 6, 7, and 8.

The Committee of Council is equally amenable to Parliament, annually, for all its proceedings : the sum confided to it is not greater than that entrusted to the Treasury. As it consists of five responsible Members of the Cabinet, instead of only one, the security for correct administration is augmented, and its proceedings are, in all respects, rendered more open to observation, by their separation from the mass of details with which the Treasury is encumbered, and their transference to a department where they can obtain more constant and deliberate attention from the Executive. In all these respects the change is a great improvement, though it appears to have been the source of much groundless alarm.

But we perceive the Archbishop of Canterbury, in the recent debate in the House of Lords, remarked, " He knew not if there was any objection in principle to the Committee appointed, but he should have thought the Lords of the Treasury were just as competent to judge of these matters as the Noble Lords named."

In his letter to the Lord President of the Council, Lord John Russell proceeds to state, that " among the first objects to which any grant may be applied, will be the establishment of a Normal School. In such a school a body of schoolmasters may be formed, competent to assume the management of similar institutions in all parts of the country. In such a school, likewise, the best modes of teaching may be introduced, and those who wish to improve the schools of their neighbourhood may have an opportunity of observing their results.

" In any Normal or Model School to be established by the Board, four principal objects should be kept in view ; namely, religious instruction, general instruction, moral training, and habits of industry. Of these four, I need only allude to the first. With respect to religious instruction, there is, as your Lordship is aware, a wide, or apparently wide difference of opinion among those who have been most forward in promoting education.

" The National Society, supported by the Established Church, contend that the schoolmaster should be invariably a Churchman ; that the Church Catechism should be taught in the school to all the scholars, that all should be required to attend church on Sundays, and that the schools should be, in every case, under the superintendence of the clergyman of the parish.

" The British and Foreign School Society, on the other hand, admit Churchmen and Dissenters equally as schoolmasters, require that the Bible should be taught in their schools, but insist that no catechism should be admitted.

" Others, again, contend that secular instruction should be the business of the school, and that the ministers of different persuasions should each instruct separately the children of their own followers.

" In the midst of these conflicting opinions, there is not practically that exclusiveness among the Church societies, nor that indifference to religion among those who exclude dogmatic instruction from the school, which their mutual accusations would lead bystanders to suppose.

" Much, therefore, may be effected by a temperate attention to the fair claims of the Established Church, and the religious freedom sanctioned by law.

"On this subject I need only say, that it is her Majesty's wish that the youth of this kingdom should be religiously brought up, and that the right of conscience should be respected."

The necessity for the immediate establishment of Normal Schools is demonstrated by the account given in the subjoined Table of the number of teachers, (engaged in daily instruction, in various classes of schools,) who had received any previous preparation for their vocation, in the five large northern towns to which we have before referred, and in Westminster.

Number of Teachers of various Classes of Day and Evening Schools, and the number who have received any Education for their Employment, in the undermentioned places :—

	Dame Schools.			Common Boys' & Girls' Schools.			Superior Private Schools.			Evening Schools.			Infant Schools.			Endowed and Charity Schools.		
	Number of Teachers.	Number educated for their employment.	Not ascertained.	Number of Teachers.	Number educated for their employment.	Not ascertained.	Number of Teachers.	Number educated for their employment.	Not ascertained.	Number of Teachers.	Number educated for their employment.	Not ascertained.	Number of Teachers.	Number educated for their employment.	Not ascertained.	Number of Teachers.	Number educated for their employment.	Not ascertained.
MANCHESTER	230	..	8	179	29	11	114	24	9	83	7	4	5	..	..	24	5	5
SALFORD	65	10	..	42	8	..	29	14	..	28	7	..	3	..	..	13	2	..
LIVERPOOL	244	2	..	194	18	2	143	71	11	43	6	..	17	1	..	50	18	7
BURY	30	2	..	17	2	..	8	6	..	6	..	..	2	..	..	4	2	..
YORK	37	..	..	23	2	..	30	10	3	2	..	..	3	1	..	31	19	3
TOTALS	606	14	8	455	59	13	324	125	23	162	20	4	30	2	..	122	46	15
WESTMINSTER, (in 3 districts) St. Martin-in-the-Fields, St. Clement Danes, St. Mary-le-Strand, St. Paul, Covent Garden, and the Savoy	21	1	5	33	9	4	32	18	2	..	..	..	5	3	1	14	7	3
St. John and St. Margaret	63	12	..	41	20	..	24	20	..	..	..	..	6	4	..	23	12	2
St. George, St. James, and St. Anne, Soho	46	7	..	55	25	..	73	54	1	..	..	..	6	5	..	18	10	..
TOTALS	130	20	5	129	54	4	129	92	3	..	..	..	17	12	1	55	29	5

Accordingly the minute of the proceedings of the Committee of Privy Council on Education, of the 11th of April, 1839, related chiefly to the plan of a Normal School. This plan was subsequently postponed, in consequence of the difficulty of obtaining a concurrence of public opinion respecting the means to be adopted for the religious instruction of the children and teachers of different religious denominations in that school. We shall only remark here, that " religion" was, in this school, " to be combined with the whole matter of instruction, and to regulate the entire system of discipline," as respected the children trained therein ; and that " the religious instruction of the candidate teachers" was " to form an essential and prominent element of their studies, and no certificate" was " to be granted, unless the authorised religious teacher" had " previously attested his confidence in the character, religious knowledge, and zeal of the candidate whose religious instruction he" had " superintended." The postponement of the establishment of a Normal School, has been represented as the temporary postponement only of this particular plan, which, notwithstanding repeated assurances to the contrary in Parliament, it is contended may still be carried into execution during the recess. A perusal of the clause of the Report of the Committee of Council of the 3rd of June, which announces the postponement of any attempt to create a Normal School, will convince any candid reader that, as the whole proceedings of the Committee are annually dependent on the opinion and votes of the House, the Committee could only have referred to the " greater concurrence of opinion," as far as it influenced the decisions of Parliament, or, in other words, to the opinion of Parliament. The postponement of any proceedings respecting the Normal School was announced in the following terms, in the Report of the Committee of Council on the third of June. :—

" The Committee are of opinion that the most useful application of any sums voted by Parliament, would consist in the employment of those moneys in the establishment of a Normal School, under the direction of the state, and not placed under the management of a voluntary Society. The Committee, however, experience so much difficulty in reconciling conflicting views respecting the provisions which they are desirous to make in furtherance of your Majesty's wish, that the children and teachers instructed in this school should be duly trained in the principles of the Christian religion, while the rights of conscience should be respected; that it is not in the power of the Committee to mature a plan for the accomplishment of this design without further consideration; and they therefore postpone taking any steps for this purpose until greater concurrence of opinion is found to prevail."

As the Committee of Council have postponed to another year the establishment of a Normal school, we shall reserve to the close of these remarks our comments on the plan which they submitted to Parliament, and we proceed to point out in what respects the plan, now proposed by the Committee of Council for the appropriation of any sums voted by Parliament for the purpose of promoting public education, differs from that formerly adopted by the Treasury.

1. " The Lords of the Committee recommend that the sum of £10,000., granted by Parliament in 1835, towards the erection of normal or model schools, be given in equal proportions to the National Society, and the British and Foreign School Society.

2. " That the remainder of the subsequent grants of the years 1837 and 1838 yet unappropriated, and any grant which may be voted in the present year, be chiefly applied in aid of subscriptions for building, and, in particular cases, for the support of schools connected with those societies, but that the rule hitherto adopted of making a grant to those places where the largest proportion is subscribed be not invariably adhered to, should application be made from very poor and populous districts, where subscriptions to a sufficient amount cannot be obtained."

Thus far no objection appears to have been raised to the plan.

3. " The Committee do not feel themselves precluded from

making grants in particular cases which shall appear to them to call for the aid of Government, although the applications may not come from either of the two mentioned societies."

The special exception thus made to the general rule may have been the source of some apprehension, and it certainly has been the subject of much misrepresentation. We find it difficult however to believe that if in any particular locality great destitution, combined with extreme ignorance and demoralization, should be found to prevail, to which the plan of either of the two societies should be found to be absolutely inapplicable without some variation in deference to the right of conscience, any reasonable man to whom authority to decide such a question was committed, having before him the minutes of the Committee of Council, would not determine it, somewhat in the following manner. The minutes of the Committee plainly limit the application of the sums voted by Parliament to schools connected with the two societies, with the exception of these particular cases. It is therefore evident that any deviation from the plans by which the two societies are distinguished from each other, and from other societies, (i. e. the method of giving religious instruction,) ought in such cases to be admitted on the plea of absolute necessity—the choice being between, on the one hand, ignorance and barbarism, and on the other the erection of a school in which a variation from the plans of the two societies is admitted, and that as the distinguishing characteristics of the two societies relate to religious instruction, this variation should be only such as would be required for the success of the school. One principle * * * * * * * * * is especially applicable to these cases, viz. that while the Government is most anxious that religious instruction should be united to secular, and will therefore grant all proper facilities for that purpose, the state is peculiarly charged with the duty of rendering secular instruction accessible to all, and with the improvement of the quality of such secular instruction by assistance from the public

* Certain words omitted. See Preface.

funds and by constant superintendence.   *   *   *

*   *   *   *   *   *   *   *

*   *   *   *   *   *   *   *

*   *   *   *   * The particular regulation embraced, in this clause of the minute of the Committee of Council, provides for a cautious experimental application of the principle as a temporary expedient. Arrangements, similar to those proposed by the Committee of the British and Foreign School, in their memorial dated 14th April, 1838, would probably suffice in such exceptional cases, viz. "That the Holy Scriptures should be read and taught in" such "schools, such instruction to form a part of the usual occupation of the school, and to be communicated by the schoolmaster, but that the children of Catholics and Jews might, if their parents required it, be absent at such time, and that the children of Dissenters should not be compelled to learn any religious formulary or catechism to which their parents objected."

4. "The Committee recommend that no further grant be made, now or hereafter, for the establishment and support of Normal schools, or of any other schools, unless the right of inspection be retained, in order to secure a conformity to the regulations and discipline established in the several schools, with such improvements as may from time to time be suggested by the Committee. A part of any grant voted in the present year may be usefully applied to the purposes of inspection, and to the means of acquiring a complete knowledge of the present state of education in England and Wales."

We have seen that the inspection of schools by a skilled agency is regarded by the Continental Governments as second only to the foundation of Normal schools in its influence on the advancement of primary education. We have observed how well organized are the arrangements for the inspection of schools in Holland. M. Cousin says, "The

Dutch legislators made no attempt at a master-piece of codi-fication, in which the whole subject of primary instruction was to be divided and classed according to the rules of philoso-phical analysis; they went straight to their point by the shortest and the safest road, and as inspection must be the funda-mental basis of primary schools, it was inspection they esta-blished by law." And in another place he says—" There are, by the law both of Prussia and Holland, salaried officers called Inspectors, selected because they are found to possess the requi-site qualifications, who are responsible to Government for the whole of the primary schools within a given district." (Their powers are, therefore, vastly more extensive than any thing contemplated in the minute of the Committee of Council). " This is the true kind of government," he adds, " for pri-mary schools, and to determine how the organization of that government shall be most skilfully contrived is, in my mind, the vital question in a system of popular education." M. Guizot, in his Report to the King of the French, on the execution of the Law of the 28th of June, 1833, attaches at least equal im-portance to this measure, and describes in detail the means by which this inspection is accomplished throughout the whole of France. Lord Lansdowne, in the debate in the House of Lords, " appealed to the experience of those Noble Lords who had sat upon the Committee of Inquiry into the state of Edu-cation in Ireland. He appealed to the experience of those Noble Lords whether they were not met at every step of their inquiry by evidence shewing that some inspection of those schools on behalf of the public was absolutely indispensable to their success as a means of education."

The subjoined evidence of the Rev. J. C. Wigram, the Se-cretary of the National School Society, and of Mr. Dunn, the Secretary of the British and Foreign School Society, leads to the same conclusion.*

* " REV. J. C. WIGRAM,

" Chairman.] Do you not think that if the Government makes grants of money for the purpose of aiding schools on either system, that they may fairly make it a

After recommending the appointment of a Board of Education, the Committee of the British and Foreign School, in a

condition that a due inspection of the schools should take place, and that adequate returns should be made to Parliament to show that the schools are well and efficiently conducted?—I think it would be very desirable that they should do so ; and I think that they might promote that object very much, and with great benefit, by giving grants in aid of some places to the schoolmasters of certain districts, upon examinations reported, with all particulars, with respect to a certain number of schools ; for instance, that a return should be made of the particulars which they might determine, respecting not less than 50 schools, and that some pecuniary reward should be given, to a different amount, to the five or six masters whose scholars were best conducted. Those examinations might be triennial, or at distant intervals, and in order to prevent the same man from always getting the reward, the prizes might be given with due reference to the circumstances of the school, and for different qualifications in the state of the school. It might be one year given for the intellectual state of the school, another year for retaining the scholars for a longer period ; and other qualifications might be introduced. It has been done by the National Society to a small extent in many parts of the country, and with great benefit."

" HENRY DUNN, ESQ.

" Do you not think that one of the first steps towards any general plan of education for the humbler classes would be, the formation of such a board as the two great parties who have interested themselves in education in this country would have confidence in ?—I think it would ; and that then their efforts should be directed to improve the existing schools rather than extend them. I should lay great stress upon that ; there are a great number of schools scattered throughout the country, of all kinds and descriptions, which, with inspection and a little assistance, might be rendered efficient schools.

" When you give an opinion as to the necessity of improving, rather than extending, existing schools, you may not have gone into the detail of the want of efficient schools in the towns of Lancashire ?—No one can have a stronger impression than I have of the want of schools ; but I believe that the improvement of schools leads to their extension.

" Do you not think that it would be very practicable, supposing by any mode a sufficient fund was provided, to do both ; that is, to improve, and at the same time gradually to extend schools for the humbler classes?—I quite think so ; but to begin by extending is, I think, to begin at the wrong end; the first step should rather be to improve, and give efficiency to those which at present exist.

" Do not you think that one necessary accompaniment of the Board to promote education would be some system of Inspectors, who should make returns to the Central Board of the degree of efficiency of the schools, and the number attending, and who should make periodical visits to inquire and look into the state of the schools ?—I think it would be essential."

Memorial addressed to Lord John Russell on the 14th of April, 1838, say

" It has been suggested that great advantages would result if these Commissioners were brought, in the disposal of the public funds into immediate correspondence with the individual or Local Committee sustaining each separate school, instead of acting through the agency of any society or societies; this point seems well worthy of consideration; but, however this may be decided, the Committee would suggest—1st. That the Board should not interfere in any way with the religious instruction imparted in any school. 2nd. That it should not impose any terms or restrictions, except such as might be necessary in order to secure efficient teaching, and an adequate share of secular information."

On this subject the Archbishop of Canterbury, in the recent debate on Education, said, " He conceived that the public when they made a grant for relief, should be assured of the efficiency of that relief. (Hear, hear.) Whenever a grant of public money was made, the public had a right to know that it had been properly applied; and he was satisfied that the public would be contented if they knew, that with the money which they had granted the secular instruction was properly applied to the people, leaving the religious instruction in the hands of the Church," (hear.) On these observations the Marquis of Lansdowne remarked, " Would the Right Reverend Prelate forgive him for stating, that it had never entered into the mind of any member of the Committee of Privy Council to use the Inspectors as agents to interfere either directly or indirectly with the religious education given in the schools? What the Inspectors ought to interfere in was the more mechanical arrangements and improvements in education—improvements which ought to be introduced into all schools, as they did not bear on any question of religion, but on a question which was all but of equal importance—he meant the training up of the scholars in those habits of discipline, of industry, and of employment, (hear, hear,) which ought to form part of every plan of general education." (Hear, hear.)

On the propriety of a system of Inspection, and on the limits to be assigned to it, one fruit of the recent discussions in Parliament seems to be a concurrence of opinion in the highest authorities, and in the representatives of the Government and the Church.

The whole discussion tends to prove the importance, not to say the necessity, of an inquiry into the state of Education in England and Wales. Our precise statistical information is limited to a few districts in which the spontaneous exertions of individuals have collected facts. The knowledge we have of the extent of destitution is general only, and therefore not satisfactory to minds accustomed to a careful induction. Such an inquiry will doubtless prove of eminent service by stimulating the spontaneous exertions of society for the extension of education, and by diffusing information to guide its newly awakened zeal. We may hope, by such means, also to obtain a more intimate acquaintance with the opinions of all classes on this momentous subject; and that the wants and moral and social peculiarities of different districts may be examined, so that when the period arrives that a more comprehensive measure can be submitted to the Legislature, it may be welcomed by a greater concurrence of popular opinion.

CHAPTER IV.

EXAMINATION OF THE MINUTE OF THE COMMITTEE OF COUNCIL OF THE 11TH OF APRIL, RESPECTING THE ESTABLISHMENT OF A NORMAL SCHOOL WHICH MINUTE IS NOW SUPERSEDED BY THAT OF THE 3RD OF JUNE.

THE most important part of the plan originally submitted by the Committee of Privy Council to Parliament, was, as we have said, abandoned in consequence of the difficulty encountered in attempting to reconcile a due regard to the legitimate claims of the Established Church with a respect for the rights of conscience. Though the establishment of a Normal School has been for the present postponed, it may be useful to shew what were the views of the Committee of Privy Council respecting the principles on which such an establishment ought to be conducted, and on the details of its internal economy. The departments of religious and general instruction, and of moral and industrial training proposed in Lord John Russell's letter to the President of the Council were included as elements of the plan of this school. It will be most convenient to consider the arrangements for religious instruction last.

The Committee of Council appear from that Minute to have been impressed with the fact, that throughout the country the number of schools for the poorer classes is inadequate to the reception of those who need instruction, but that this defect, from its extent and notoriety, appears to withdraw attention in some degree, from the equally lamentable inefficiency of the teachers commonly employed in the primary schools, arising from their imperfect attainments, their ignorance of correct methods of instruction, and still more from their want of skill in training the habits and developing the characters of the children, so as to prepare them for the persevering discharge of their duties in life. In many cases, the profession of the educator has fallen into the hands of persons who are destitute of means, not merely from want of ability, but from defects of character, and who resort to this calling after they have been proved to be unfit for any other. The exertions of the Clergy and Ministers in the religious instruction of the population would be materially assisted if the instruction of the children of the poor were given in such a form as not merely to inform their minds on their duties to God and to man, but to influence their habits and feelings, so that a sense of the true source of all moral and social obligations, might be not merely instilled as a precept on the understanding, but be imbibed from every part of the daily routine in such a way as to influence the life. It is feared, that the teachers now employed, often content themselves with requiring that the approved formularies be committed to memory.

In order to abate these evils the Committee of Council intended to found a school in which candidates might acquire knowledge necessary to the exercise of their future profession, and be practised in the most approved methods, both of moral training and instruction.

By such means alone can the parochial, village, and town schools, as well as the endowed and charity and private schools throughout the country be supplied with teachers duly impressed with the great responsibilities of their vocation—entering on the discharge of their functions, as on a mission of truth and civilization—and furnished with such attainments, such skill in the practice of their art—with minds and habits so disciplined as to fit them to become at once the guides and the companions, the instructors and the foster parents of the children whose temporal and eternal welfare is committed to their care.

Such a school necessarily included a Model School in which children might be taught and trained, and it appeared expedient that it should comprise children of all ages from three to fourteen, in sufficient numbers to form an Infant School, as well as schools for children above seven. A considerable portion of the children were to board and lodge in the establishment, in order that the means of moral training might be proportionately more complete, and opportunities afforded to the candidate teachers for acquiring a knowledge of the method of regulating the moral condition of such a household greater than any which could be obtained in a school attended solely or chiefly by day scholars.

The Model School, thus formed, would have afforded examples, of approved methods of instruction in each stage of proficiency and in each department of knowledge. The earliest information of alimp rovements would have been obtained ; they would have been systematically examined, and introduced when approved, in that form which might appear to render them most easily applicable to the wants of the country. Industrial and moral training were to be developed, so as constantly to give a practical tendency to the entire instruction of the school, supplying the future handicraftsman, or domestic servant, with the knowledge required in his station, and reducing precept to habit.

The Model and Normal School were to have been beneath the superintendence of a Rector, acting under the regulation of the Committee of Council. The selection of Teachers and of candidates for the office of teacher would have been a subject of great difficulty and importance. Diligent inquiry, under direction of the Committee of the Privy Council, concerning their previous habits and associations, an examination of their attainments, evidence of gentleness of disposition, and a fondness for the duties of an educator, together with a sense of the secular and religious responsibility of the office, would have been essential preliminaries to the admission of a candidate teacher.

The internal organization of the Model School indicates the method of instruction which was to have been adopted. The Committee of Council proposed to arrange the classes in separate rooms, or sections of the same apartment, divided by partitions, so as to enable the simultaneous method to be applied to forty or fifty children of similar proficiency. The Committee intended also to use the gallery, commonly employed only in the Infant School, as a means of giving lessons on objects of sense, or requiring illustrations from objects of sense, to the older children in larger bodies than when assembled in the classes for mere technical instruction. The gallery would also have been used at periods when the teacher desired to assemble the children for serious moral admonition. Such arrangements would have enabled each teacher not merely to convey his instructions with greater success, shut out from the noise and confusion incident to the assemblage of large numbers in the same room, but to have cultivated moral relations with his scholars, who would gradually have learned to regard him with affection as well as respect, resulting from the paternal character of the discipline. All the lessons in which it is important that the sympathies should be awakened, as well as the understanding, might be conveyed by the teacher in a more impressive manner in a separate apartment than in the large hall of a school filled with some hundreds of children. Without such arrangements, the design of the Committee of Council to interweave moral training with the whole tissue of instruction would not have been fulfilled; and the teachers must have been content with whatever success they could attain in the merely *intellectual* advancement of their pupils.

The simultaneous instruction which the Committee of Council apparently intended to combine with the monitorial or mutual instruction prevalent in this country, depends for its efficacy on the fact that, by the simultaneous method, the mind of the teacher may be more constantly in contact with that of every child under his care. The moral agencies employed are, under such a method, greatly superior to those in operation where the child receives instruction chiefly, if not wholly, from a boy but little older than himself.

The successful prosecution of the simultaneous method supposes that the teacher is accustomed to a careful analysis of the subjects of instruction to their simplest elements, and that he proceeds by a suggestive method from the previous limits of the child's knowledge, that is, from the most simple and rudimentary facts to those which are the result of combination. In this process each step is accompanied by a corresponding exercise of the child's mind, which finds a natural pleasure in pursuing a process of induction stimulating it to exertion. To learn is no longer a task, but a pleasure; the teacher successfully appeals to the sense of utility and the natural desire to know and combine, which are ordinarily discouraged by the difficulties attending an opposite method. The discipline of the school naturally acquires a milder character with willing pupils than with the sluggish or perverse; and the educator depends on his skill in rendering the pursuit of knowledge attractive, rather than on a resort to the inferior stimulus of rewards and punishments.

The Committee were of opinion that industrial instruction forms an important element of the routine of a Model School, probably not only because it practically inculcates the great lesson of industry, but also because it tends to give a special character to the matter of instruction in the school, keeping it in close relation with the condition of workmen and servants, and engrafting whatever is new on habits and pursuits which are necessary and permanent.

The candidate teachers were to reside in the Normal School in order that their habits and characters might be under the constant observation of the Rector and his assistant teachers.

The class-rooms were to be so constructed as to afford the candidate teachers an opportunity of attending the lessons without distracting the attention of the children or of the teacher.

Means were to be provided for the instruction of the candidate teachers in the theory of their art, and for furnishing them with whatever knowledge is requisite for success in it.

The superintendence of their studies and the general regulation of their conduct would have devolved on the Rector of the School. He would have given lectures on the method and matter of instruction, and the whole art of training children of the poor. Each course of study would have been conducted by him, as well as the reading, and the exercise and examination of the candidate teachers. The order in which they were admitted to the practice of their art in the school, and at length entrusted with the conjoint management of the classes, together with their ultimate examination and certificate, would have been chiefly regulated by him.

The candidate teachers were to conform to such regulations respecting the internal economy of the household, as might have been issued by the Rector with the approval of the Committee of Privy Council.

In the Model School it would have been desirable to have had accommodation for at least 450 children, who should lodge in the household, viz. 120 infants, 200 boys and girls receiving ordinary instruction, and 50 boys and 50 girls receiving special instruction, leaving 30 children absent from sickness or other causes. Such arrangements would have enabled the teachers to conduct the school with complete success on the best methods, and thus to afford to the candidate teachers the best opportunity of acquiring the art of teaching.

But in order to enable the teachers to realize the application of these methods under all the limitations and obstructions which must arise in a small village or town day-school, it was deemed desirable that a day school of 150 or 200 children, of all ages and both sexes, should form part of the establishment.

Here the candidate teacher would have learned the limitations which the organization and method pursued in the larger school must undergo when the numbers are reduced, and when all ages are assembled in the same room: and would have become acquainted with the expedients to be adopted under varying circumstances; for example, when the number was even still further reduced by the prevalence of sickness, by the inclemency of the weather, or by the caprice of parents. He would have been taught how to communicate with the parents respecting the conduct, health, and progress of their children—respecting the payment of the school fees, the management of the children at home, and their observance of their religious duties morning and evening and on the Sunday. The industrial training of children in day schools also has some peculiarities, and their moral training is liable to interference from the parents and other external circumstances, over which the teacher has little control, and is certainly limited in its operation to the period spent in the school and exercise ground.

The progress of education would probably soon, under the influence of the Normal School, have multiplied the number of Rural Schools of Industry, so as to have enabled the candidate teachers to visit other Model Schools near the metropolis, where they might have completed their acquaintance with the modifications, required by limitations and obstructions incidental to the different situations of the schools. The teachers having charge of schools in London and its vicinity might have been admitted to the Rector's lectures, and to certain of his classes.

Teachers having charge of schools, whether in the metropolis or elsewhere, might, during the holidays common to such establishments, have been permitted to attend the school.

Conferences of teachers trained in the Seminary would probably have occurred, under regulations issued by the Committee of Privy Council; at those conferences the Rector might have presided—the teachers might have given an account of their schools, of the difficulties which they had encountered and overcome, and especially of any improvement in apparatus or method, &c. of sufficient importance for consideration.

That the benefits derivable from such an Institution are almost incalculably great appears to be universally admitted. The want of teachers thus furnished with all the acquirements necessary for their honourable station—thus trained in correct methods of teaching—with habits of thought and demeanour so disciplined as to enable them to sustain a moral dignity while they mingle with the sports, sympathize with the feel-ngs, yet elevate the thoughts of children—capable of making knowledge attractive by the simplicity and kindness with which it is imparted—imbued with a deep sense of their religious responsibilities, and hallowing all their moral instruction by a constant reference to the sanctions of religion—the want of such men is felt by every clergyman and gentleman who takes an interest in the condition of the labouring families on his estates, and by every member of the middle classes who recognizes in the present condition of the poor proofs of the fatal void in our national institutions.

Deeply therefore do we regret the difficulty experienced in devising any method by which the religious instruction of children and teachers can be reconciled in such an establishment with due regard to the right of conscience.

The regulations contained in the Minute of the Committee of Council of the 11th of April, 1839, now superseded, were—

" Religious instruction to be considered as general and special.

" Religion to be combined with the whole matter of instruction, and to regulate the entire system of discipline.

" Periods to be set apart for such peculiar doctrinal instruction as might be required for the religious training of the children.

" To appoint a chaplain to conduct the religious instruction of children whose parents or guardians belong to the Established Church.

" The parent or natural guardian of any other child to be permitted to secure the attendance of the licensed minister of his own persuasion, at the period appointed for special religious instruction, in order to give such instruction apart.

" To appoint a licensed minister to give such special religious instruction, wherever the number of children in attendance on the Model School belonging to any religious body dissenting from the Established Church, is such as to appear to this Committee to require such special provision.

" A portion of every day to be devoted to the reading of the Scriptures in the school, under the general direction of the

Committee, and superintendence of the Rector.—Roman Catholics, if their parents or guardians require it, to read their own version of the Scriptures, either at the time fixed for reading the Scriptures, or at the hours of special instruction."

These regulations had reference to the religious instruction of the children in the Model School only, and it was not the intention of the Committee of Council to propose similar regulations for the adoption of any other school—much less was this school intended in this respect as a type of schools to be established in different parts of the country. On the contrary, the sum voted by the Committee of the House of Commons was to have been distributed to schools in connection with the National and the British and Foreign School Societies, with certain exceptional cases only, admitted in consequence of the inapplicability of the rules of those societies in neighbourhoods where extreme ignorance and destitution appeared to demand the interference of Government for the civilization of the people.

The Committee of Privy Council appear to have considered it unnecessary to descend into an explanation of all the more minute regulations by which the instruction of the children in the principles of the Christian religion was to have been guarded; but their views appear in all their leading features to be so strictly in accordance with those of that able and pious prelate, Daniel Wilson, the Bishop of Calcutta, as developed in regulations which he proposed to the Committee of the Martinière, that we feel bound to state the most material parts of those regulations.

This institution owed its existence to the following extraordinary circumstances. An English private soldier by great merit rose from the ranks in India—was promoted to the rank of Major-General—and amassed a great fortune. At his death he bequeathed his wealth for general education, without reference to the creed of those who partook of the benefits of the institution to be founded.

It was the wish of the Bishop of Calcutta to have founded this institution on the express doctrines and discipline of the

Church of England only; but finding that the intentions of the founder were that the benefits of the institution should be extended to all persons, without distinction of creed, he proposed and strenuously advocated the plan described in the report, comprehending, as he says, " all the great doctrines of redemption, as held by the *five main* divisions *of the Christian world—the English, the Scotch, the Roman Catholic, the Greek, and the Armenian churches—as our fundamental principles, leaving the minister of each church to supply instructions on the sacraments and matters of discipline to the children of their own communions respectively.*" The following are extracts from the report, signed by the Committee, and adopted unanimously by the Board, and we may add, republished by the Bishop in his own vindication.

" *Report, &c. of the Committee appointed to frame a Plan, &c.*

" I. Your Committee submit, that in order to meet the first rule adopted by the Honourable Governors, the religious instruction of the children must be divided into two parts; *the one general, the other particular;* the one embracing the fundamental truths of Christianity, as they are held in common by the five great existing divisions of Christendom enumerated in the rule; the other relating to discipline, church government, the sacraments, and other matters on which differences more or less important exist. Your Committee consider that the first part should be taught daily and publicly to all the children by the head master of the school; the second, privately, and on particular days, by the ministers and teachers whom the parents of the respective children may, with the approbation of the Governors, select.

" II. The following are the main truths held in common, on which the public religious instruction should, in your Committee's opinion, proceed.

1. The Being of God; his unity and perfections.

2. The Holy Scriptures of the Old and New Testament, a revelation inspired by the Holy Ghost.

3. The mystery of the adorable Trinity.

4. The Deity, Incarnation, Atonement, and Intercession of our Lord and Saviour Jesus Christ.

5. The fall and corruption of man; his accountableness and guilt.

6. Salvation through grace by the meritorious sacrifice and redemption of Christ.

7. The personality and Deity of the Holy Spirit, and his operations and grace in the sanctification of man.

8. The indispensable obligation of repentance towards God, faith in Christ, and continual prayer for the grace of the Holy Spirit.

9. The moral duties which every Christian is bound to perform towards God, his neighbour, and himself, as they are summed up in the Ten Commandments, and enlarged upon in other parts of the Holy Scriptures; all based on the doctrines above specified, and enforced as their proper fruits.

" III. As to the first of these branches of the religious instruction—the public and general—the Committee recommend that it be chiefly drawn from the Holy Scriptures themselves; such simple instruction being given by the masters and mistresses in a catechetical form as may be adapted to the capacities of the children, on the points which fall within the limits of the public teaching; all matters which belong to the private, or which touch on controversy, being sedulously avoided.

" With respect to versions of the Scriptures, your Committee will offer their opinion under a subsequent rule.

" V. The second branch of the religious instruction—the private and particular—will require no regulations from your Committee; it will be merely supplementary; so that what is, in the judgment of the parents and guardians of the respective children, omitted, or insufficiently taught in public, may thus be supplied. In this private teaching the entire Catechisms of the different churches, and the versions of the Holy Scriptures approved by them, may of course be freely used.

" VII. We come next to the subject of family devotional exercises, and the public worship of Almighty God.

The daily morning and evening family prayers, your Committee suggest, should be read by the Head Master, from a Form of Prayer extracted from different liturgies, which we have prepared, and which accompanies these rules. On these occasions all the children of both sexes, and all the masters and mistresses, with all the Christian members of the household, should attend.

The family devotions should not exceed ten or fifteen minutes altogether in length.

The masters and mistresses are to allow also a few minutes to the children for private prayer, before they retire to bed at night, and when they rise in the morning.

On Sunday mornings, your Committee think all the children should be conducted to their respective churches and chapels, for the worship of the Almighty, in the manner and after the rites approved by their parents.

On Sunday evenings they recommend that the ordinary family devotions be read, with the addition of a suitable sermon, to be approved of by the governors.

The same to be done also on Sunday mornings, when circumstances may prevent the children from going out; with the addition of a Litany extracted from one or more of the Liturgies of different churches.

" VIII. As it respects versions of the Holy Scriptures, your Committee are not aware that the Greek and Armenian churches have any English version of their own. The English and Scotch churches use the authorised English version. It remains only that the case of the church of Rome be considered, which has long possessed an English version of its own— that of Douay and Rheims : we recommend that, whenever the Roman Catholic children are required to have the Holy Scriptures in their hands, and to learn lessons, or receive direct religious instruction from them, this version be permitted to be employed ; the copies being, of course, without notes or indexes which touch on controversy, and the master taking care to range the children in different classes, so that no confusion may arise by the variations in the readings.

' "As this, however, could not be done in family prayer, where all the children of all classes and each sex, as well as the Christian household, are assembled together, we are of opinion that the portions of Holy Scripture, directed to be read as a part of the doctrines, should be taken from the authorised English version : the selection being, of course, subject to the provisions of the foregoing rules.

" Your Committee do not know that they need proceed more into detail. Much will and ought to be left to the head master, if he be a man of piety, talent, discretion, and temper. His suggestions, founded on experience, will be of the greatest value. Much will also depend on the number, description, age, and capacities of the children. But your Committee feel a great confidence that by this union of public and religious instruction, on the basis of the great doctrines of redemption held by the universal church, with the private inculcation of what regards church discipline, the sacraments, and other matters of controversy, *the practical blessings of a Christian education may be conveyed to the children, without indifference and latitudinarianism on the one hand, or a spirit of debate and proselytism on the other.*

" Daniel Calcutta.

" Robert S. Leger, V. A.

" James Charles."

"*August* 31, 1835."

It is scarcely necessary to add, that this Report is not inserted in this place, on the presumption that it anticipates in all its details the plan which the Committee of Council had prepared. On the contrary, we have already been publicly informed, that on no occasion did the Committee of Council intend that different versions of the Scriptures should be used *in the same apartment* in the Model School, but only in separate rooms. We need not more particularly allude to other details upon which the Committee of Council have expressed no opinion; but we have quoted these extracts from this report of the Committee of the Martinière, to show that one of the ablest and most pious prelates that ever shed the lustre of a comprehensive and highly cultivated mind and of eminent Christian virtues on society and the church, has lent the authority of his name to regulations conceived in the same spirit of Christian charity, as that part of the minute of the Committee of Council of the 11th of April, by which the religious instruction of the children in the Model School was to be regulated. By such means the Bishop of Calcutta believes " the practical blessings of a Christian education may be conveyed to the children without indifference and latitudinarianism on the one hand, or a spirit of debate and proselytism on the other."

This Report may at least serve as a complete answer to the question which the Archbishop of Canterbury asked in the House of Lords, respecting "the meaning of general instruction in Christianity." We refer him to the Bishop of Calcutta's solution of that question.

" Then as to the minute, ' Religion to be combined with the whole matter of instruction, and to regulate the entire system of discipline,'" the Archbishop said, " he was at a loss how this was to be carried into effect." The answer is contained in the Report signed by the Bishop of Calcutta.

On this question, the Bishop of London quoted the opinion of Professor Thiersch respecting the seminary of teachers at Kayerslautern. We solicit our reader's attention to the very passage which the Right Reverend Prelate read to the House of Lords. The Professor, on whom the Bishop passed so just an eulogium, respects the ennobling sentiments of Christian charity which induced the Government, in the circle of the Rhine, to establish a common seminary for teachers. " In the Bavarian circle of the Rhine," he says, " there is but one seminary for teachers. This is too little, both for the number of pupils to be instructed and for the wants of different confessions. It was rightly observed to me at the training seminary of Neuwied by its excellent director, Braun, that an institution of this kind flourishes better the more nearly it approximates to a family circle, and as its object is not so much instruction as education, that about thirty-six is the largest number it should contain. Besides, many arguments recommend the division of the seminary according to confessions of faith. I know and respect the motives which dictated that, in the circle of the Rhine, both confessions (Protestant and Romanist) should be united in a single seminary, in the advantages of which even the future rabbies should be allowed to participate. But it is conceivable, and the experience of other countries shows that it is found, that when seminaries are divided, toleration may be secured both among teachers and communities; indeed, that this is more effectually attained, the more each confession is secured in its real wants. Among these wants it would seem that the education and instruction of the persons to whom elementary schools are to be intrusted must be especially included; and since such an education cannot be conceived unless its basis is firmly laid in the knowledge of some Christian confession, therefore the division of seminaries according to modes of faith, as happens in Nassau, in Prussia, and perhaps one may say in every other country, is necessarily required." Apparently adopting the erroneous opinion that the plan of religious instruction proposed for the Model School only, was to be extended to other schools, the Bishop also referred, in support of his argument, to the opinion of M. Guizot, when, as Minister of Public Instruction in France, he was entrusted with the execution of the law of the 28th of June 1833. This opinion was extracted from a circular addressed to the French Prefets on the 24th of July 1833. The Bishop quoted only part of the paragraph of the circular relating to this question; we will give the whole, and we shall then request our readers' attention to the opinion of M. Cousin in his report to the Chamber of Peers, as the head of the Commission charged with the examination of the " Projet de Loi" on Primary instruction in 1833. M. Guizot says, " In those communes in which the inhabitants profess different forms of religion recognized by the state, schools particularly attached to each of these religious denominations may be established with consent of the Municipal Council, and under my authorization. It is, in general, desirable that children whose parents do not profess the same religious opinions, should early contract, by frequenting the same schools, those habits of natural good will and tolerance which will grow into sentiments of justice and union when they become fellow citizens. It may, however, sometimes be necessary, even with a view to the public peace that separate schools should be opened in the same commune for each faith." So far the Bishop, who omitted what follows, " You will be careful to transmit to me before the fifth of September a report of the deliberations of the Municipal Councils on this subject, with your suggestions. It will possibly happen that in some communes of mixed faith, the elections will have sent to the Municipal Council men only of one religious denomination and the Councils thus formed might shew themselves inclined to support only one school, notwithstanding local circumstances, such as old and deeply rooted dissensions—the importance of the population, or some other cause, might render the opening of a second school very desirable. I recommend you to examine with the greatest care the remonstrances which may be made against the designs of the Municipal Councils. You will communicate with them to ascertain their opinion—you will then send it to me with your own, and you will inform me what is the number of inhabitants belonging to each religious community, as well as all the facts necessary to illustrate the decision I shall have to form.

" Bear in mind, M. le Prefet, that the efficacy, as well as the liberty of religious education, and the security of families in this respect, are the principal considerations which ought to guide the administration in this matter."

We find nothing here but a provision against the intolerance of a dominant sect, which might abuse the regulations of the communal school, so as to make its religious instruction agree chiefly, if not solely, with its own views, and be a subject of vexation or suspicion to the other religious persuasions.

But we may learn from M. Cousin's report to the Chamber of Peers in what spirit the Law of primary instruction in

France was conceived. Concerning article 2, the Commission say they "cannot but applaud the homage rendered to liberty of conscience, and to the sacred rights of parents, by the declaration, that the wishes of parents shall always be consulted and complied with in whatever concerns the participation of their children in religious instruction."

Again—" The ninth article of the projet of the Government attached at least one public elementary school to each commune; and it is evident that to compel a commune to have *one*, was not forbidding it to have *several*, if it could maintain them; and that in this case the children of the commune should be distributed in the best way possible. A vast number of urban communes have several schools; and then, instead of dispersing though them all the children of different communions, it is the constant practice of the local authorities to collect the children of one communion in one school, whenever they are numerous enough to compose a whole school, and the local resources allow it. The Chamber of Deputies has deemed this practice sufficiently important to find a place in the law. This is a fresh homage to religious liberty, to which we subscribe; and we propose to adopt the amendment of the Chamber of Deputies, wording it as follows:—' In case local circumstances permit, the Minister of public instruction may, after hearing the Municipal Council, authorise, as communal schools, the schools more peculiarly attached to any one of the modes of public worship recognized by the State.'

" Thus, when there is but one school, all sects will frequent it, and will there receive a common instruction which, without injury to religious liberty (placed under the perpetual security of Article 2), will strengthen the ties which ought to unite all the children of the same country. Whenever there are several schools in a commune, the several sects shall be divided; but these different schools shall all be established on the same footing, and with the same title: they shall all enjoy the same dignity, and all the inhabitants of the commune shall contribute to their common support; as, in a higher sphere, all the citizens contribute to the general tax which goes to the maintenance of the different churches. This measure of perfect tolerance appears to us conformable to the true spirit of religion ; favourable to the public peace, worthy of the intelligence of our age and of the munificence of a great nation."

Now it cannot be too constantly borne in mind that the regulations of the Committee of Privy Council respecting the religious instruction of children of different sects in one school, related only to the Model School, and that as we have said before, the Committee (with rare exceptions admitted on the plea of urgent necessity only) intended to confine the application of the money voted by Parliament to the assistance of schools connected with the National Society, and the British and Foreign School Society. The Bishop of London's argument was therefore addressed against a plan which was not contained in the minutes of the Committee of Privy Council, and to represent which as within their contemplation, would be an unwarrantable assumption. But if the spirit of the French Law, to which the Right Reverend Prelate appealed, be in harmony with his Lordship's views, we shall rejoice to reckon so able an advocate among the champions of civil and religious liberty.

The inferences which Professor Pillans draws from the practice of the German states to which the Bishop of London referred, and from the circular addressed by M. Guizot to the Prefets of France, —are exactly the opposite of those which the Bishop of London conceives himself entitled to make. As we have quoted the extracts alluded to by the Right Reverend Prelate, we place in contrast with his inferences those of the able Head Master of the High School, and now Professor of Humanity in the University of Edinburgh.

" Are you aware what is the system in Germany in that respect (of religion) ?—I should say the arrangements in Germany upon that subject are extremely liberal, and, with every anxiety for religious instruction, provide at the same time for the cases of different religion with the greatest attention, and with the most perfect impartiality.

" Do you not suppose that a sufficient religious education could be conveyed without the conveyance, at the same time, of any peculiar religious doctrine?—I am disposed to think so as regards children, both because I think that the doctrines of our religion, as far as they have a tendency to influence the habits and practice of the young, may be separated and kept distinct from the peculiar opinions of any one sect, and because such opinions embodied in any school books, I should consider as nearly ineffectual for any purpose at all, turning, as they generally do, upon points which are altogether beyond the comprehension of the young mind ; and therefore it is that I think it most of all desirable to have a system of religious instruction, for schools founded upon the Scriptures, but directed only to those parts of the sacred volume which have a moral tendency, and which are likely to influence the conduct, cherish the best affections, and regulate the behaviour of the young. I am fortified in that opinion by the example of the German States, where the school instruction is founded on this principle, as well as of France, where the law on that head is very nearly a transcript of the German.

" Has it ever suggested itself to you, in the matter of teaching religion, that teaching theology is one thing, and inculcating religious habits is another?—Yes, I think that is obvious, though certainly not sufficiently attended to in practice.

" In the creation of religious habits, do not all sorts of Christians agree, as far as you have had an opportunity of considering the subject of teaching?—I think so.

" Supposing that we wanted to teach theology to pupils, the teaching of theology would be like the teaching of any other science ?—It certainly requires a matured understanding to deal with subjects so deep and difficult ; nor can it be a very profitable employment for the mind of a child, to be turned to points of doctrine upon which, from its very nature, it cannot be informed.

" So that, in fact, the business of a teacher of the people, considering the matter of national education, would be to form religious habits, and those might be formed in a national school which did not impose any dogmata upon the minds of the pupils? —I should say so certainly; at the same time I wish it to be understood that by dogmata I mean the peculiar tenets of any particular sect: the leading and distinctive doctrines of Christianity ought not to be omitted. It is these only, I conceive, that are within the province of the schoolmaster, his vocation being more of a literary than of an ecclesiastical character.

" Assuming that there is a general coincidence in all Christian sects, those truths might be taught in a national school, without trenching upon any religious differences that might exist between them?—I think they might.

" And, therefore, if there were a spirit of forbearance among the Christian sects at this time existing in England, there would, in reality, be no objection on this score to the institution of a national education?—Not the least, I should think. There is in the present day, as far as I have observed, less of excitement and mutual hostility between the different sects in Germany and France than in England; and, accordingly, in the ministerial and official instructions sent out to the prefect of the circle or department, as well as to the teachers themselves, they are strongly enjoined to encourage mixed schools, where the children may practically learn the principle of toleration and mutual forbearance, and where that cannot be done, the authorities are invited to take every means to provide such religious instruction apart as shall be thought necessary, or even to form separate schools. The last, however, they consider as a resource not to be resorted to, unless all means of uniting the two persuasions shall be found unavailing.

" Do you not suppose that the teaching of various sects in one school, under that system of Catholic faith, if it may be so called, would very much tend to promote general kindliness amongst the whole population?—I think so desirable an object most likely to be attained by such a joint and mixed system. Judging both from reason and experience, I should say it is a result that could scarcely fail to take place.

" Do you not think a true Christian feeling would be created by such a system of National Education?—I do.

" Do you consider that, in any way, the interests of religion would be injured by such a system?—On the contrary, it appears to me that the amount of religious feeling, and true Christianity wonld be increased very considerably by such an arrangement, inasmuch as we are all taught to believe, and cannot help believing, who are familiar with the Scriptures and the New Testament, that brotherly love is the first of Christian virtues."

The religious instruction of the candidate teachers in the normal school was, by the regulations of the Committee of Privy Council, to be in strict conformity with the tolerant principles which have characterised our modern legislation.

The regulation contained in the Minute of the 14th April was as follows, " The religious instruction of all candidate teachers, connected with the Established Church to be committed to the chaplain, and the special religious instruction to be committed (in any case in which a wish to that effect is expressed) to the licensed Minister of the religious persuasion of the candidate teacher, who is to attend the school at stated periods, to assist and examine the candidate teachers in their reading on religious subjects, and to afford them spiritual advice."

Let us inquire whether the Dissenters of England are entitled to so much respect in the regulations of a normal school. We may ascertain their title to consideration by examining the degree in which they have spontaneously assumed the charge of the primary education of the people of this country. If we find them in charge of a considerable amount of the primary education at present provided for the people, those who will not listen to right may perhaps be inclined to bend to necessity ; or those who refuse to admit the principle must contrive to dispose of the fact. And here, we again find ourselves greatly indebted to the labours of the London and Manchester Statistical Societies. In the towns of Manchester, Salford, Liverpool,

Bury, York, and Birmingham, comprising an estimated population of 713,000 inhabitants, the following table exhibits the number of children receiving instruction in the Sunday schools of different religious classes, and also affords similar information respecting the three divisions of Westminster, comprising 215,000 inhabitants.

	Manchester, Salford, Liverpool, Bury, York, and Birmingham.			Westminster in Three Divisions.		
	No. of Schools.	No. of Scholars on book.	Average attendance.	No. of Schools.	No. of Scholars on book.	Average attendance.
Church Establishment .	93	26,629	21,324	14	2,115	1,517
Dissenters	171	49,675	39,412	26	4,152	2,794
Catholics	16	5,686	4,563	—	—	—
Unconnected with any Religious Body . . .	4	672	513	—	—	—
Total	284	82,662	65,812	40	6267	4311

NOTE. In the case of Birmingham, the average attendance is not specified, it is therefore presumed to be the same as the number of scholars on books.

The number of Sunday schools in these towns under the Church Establishment was 107, under Dissenters 197, under Catholics 16, unconnected with any religious body 4. The average attendance of scholars at the Church schools was 22,841, at those of Dissenters 42,206, at Catholic schools 4,563, and at schools unconnected with any religious body 513.

The table referred to in the note contains these facts in detail for the five northern towns.*

The religious profession of the teachers of the various classes of day and evening schools in Manchester, Salford, Liverpool, Bury and York, and in Westminster, is shewn in the following summary, proving to what extent Dissenters have charge of the common daily instruction of the children of the middle and lower classes, in the great towns of this country.

* See Appendix, Table No. IV.

	NORTHERN TOWNS.					WESTMINSTER.				
	Number of Teachers.	Established Church.	Catholics.	Dissenters.	Not Ascertained.	Number of Teachers.	Established Church.	Catholics.	Dissenters.	Not Ascertained.
Dame Schools	606	285	62	240	19	130	97	—	29	4
Common boys' & girls' Schools	455	209	60	163	23	129	100	2	22	5
Superior boys' & girls' Schools	324	177	11	130	6	129	110	—	17	2
Infant Schools	30	18	1	11	—	17	12	—	5	—
Charity and Endowed Schools	119	74	8	34	3	55	36	2	14	3
Evening Schools	165	67	24	65	9	—	—	—	—	—
Total	1699	830	166	643	60	460	355	4	87	·14

In the above classes of schools, out of 2159 teachers, 1185 were members of the Established Church ; 170 were Catholics ; and 730 Dissenters ; while the religious profession of 74 teachers was not ascertained.

We are indebted to the Reports of the Commissioners of Inquiry into the condition of the Hand-loom weavers for the following statement of the condition of popular education in the city of Coventry, and the contiguous weaving districts of the ribbon manufacture, as collected by their secretary, Joseph Fletcher, Esq.

Remarks Explanatory of the Accompanying Table.
SEE APPENDIX.

" From the accompanying table it will be seen,

" 1st. That the population of the City and Weaving District of Coventry in 1831, was somewhat more than 55,000, and must now, therefore, reckoning on an increase of 15 per cent. which that of the previous period more than justifies, be no less than 63,000.

" 2nd. That the number of healthy children, *from two to fourteen years of age,* which the modern prevalence of Dame and Infant Schools in our manufacturing districts, marks as the limits of the school ages, is therefore about 15,000, or nearly one-fourth of the population; the proportion of those from 5 to 15 in the City and County of the City in 1821, being between one-fifth and one-fourth, according to the Census.

" 3rd. That besides the children of the richer classes at the City Free Grammar School, and about twenty-five private schools, there are 9,369 children receiving instruction of some kind, so that the total number of children receiving instruction will be about *two-thirds* of those from two to fourteen years of age, while the other *third* are under no school discipline whatever, even on the Sabbath.

" 4th. That of the total number receiving instruction, only 2,957, or scarcely *one-third*, receive any whatever in *private* schools, at the cost of their parents; and of this number, excepting the children who attend the very few pay schools which give an instruction similar that of the ordinary Lancasterian Schools, *nearly the whole* are in Dame Schools, or subscription nurseries, of the most wretched description, in which little attempt at religious instruction is made, (though sometimes the Catechisms of different creeds are found in the same schools;) and which are best described by their usual name of " out-of-the-way Schools," from the children being sent to them chiefly to be out of the way of their parents or of harm.

" 5th. That 6,412, or more than *two-thirds* of the children receiving any instruction, RECEIVE ONLY PUBLIC INSTRUCTION, which is already, therefore, a permanent institution, though on the voluntary system.

" 6th. That of this public instruction, nearly two-thirds is, at the present moment, *in the hands of Dissenters*, with some few *Roman Catholics*, under whose management 4,123 of these children are receiving all the schooling which they obtain; leaving only 2,289 under the management of the *Church*.

" 7th. That of the children receiving public instruction, 4,150, or nearly *two-thirds*, are under only *Sunday School* teaching, which is chiefly religious, and, as a means of secular instruction, almost beneath notice; and of the total number of children receiving *only* this Sunday schooling, 3,415, or nearly *seven-eighths*, are in the Schools of Dissenters; the predominance being yet greater in the country districts than in the city.

" 8th. That 1,510 children, or nearly *one-fourth* of those receiving public instruction, attend *unendowed* Day Schools, of the character of National Schools generally, with some few Infant Schools, in which the number of children attending those under the management of Dissenters, is, in the city of Coventry, approaching *two to one* of those attending the Church Schools; while in the Rural Districts, the poverty and dispersion of the Dissenting population, leave the *daily* instruction almost wholly to the Church Schools; and the *total* of children receiving instruction in public Day Schools, supported by voluntary subscriptions in the city and rural parishes jointly is therefore divided between the Church Schools and the Dissenting Schools, in nearly the reverse proportion that is observed in the city.

"9th. That the *whole* of the remaining 752 children receiving public daily instruction, are in schools more or less well *endowed*, of a character in few instances superior to National Schools, and nearly all under the management of Churchmen; and it is by the addition of these alone that the Church acquires a decided preponderance of 846, even in regard to the number of *day* scholars, to meet the overwhelming balance of nearly 3,000 in the exclusively Sunday teaching.

" 11th. That secular instruction, at all worthy of the name, being attempted only in the public Day Schools, and the few common Day Schools of superior character, the proportion of children under instruction to the population is rather 1 in 20 than 1 in 6, as the mere enumeration of the scholars of every class would indicate; an enumeration assuredly in excess, through the prevalent desire of teachers to represent their schools in the best light.

" 12th. That much has been done by these several classes of schools towards redeeming the labouring population of this district from a state approaching to absolute barbarism, cannot be doubted; any more than that somewhat of this has been pursued in a spirit of rivalry, where much more might have been accomplished by united efforts.

"And 13th. That there is still a want of any sufficient influence by which the rising generation of this district can be preserved from pursuing the like courses, and abiding in the same rudeness and misery which has been the usual lot of their predecessors.

"JOSEPH FLETCHER."

"3, *Trafalgar Square, Westminster,*
"*July* 1, 1839."

In the purely rural districts the Dissenters are not numerous. The inhabitants of agricultural parishes consist for the most part of the proprietors, the clergy, the farmers, and the labourers. Dissent has spread chiefly among the middle classes; but exceedingly less among the farmers than the inhabitants of towns. The gentry and clergy have little encouragement or assistance from the farmers in the erection or improvement of schools. The common argument employed by the farmer is, that he had little or no instruction himself, and that he does not see why his labourers' children should be as well instructed as his own. No general sympathy in the improvement of the education of agricultural labourers can be expected, until proprietary schools for the children of farmers have been established, and we hope that every intelligent landowner, and especially our aristocracy, will recognize the importance of thus providing such an education for farmers' children as shall enable the next generation to keep exact accounts of the income and outlay of their farms —to comprehend the mechanical improvements recently introduced into husbandry—to read with profit the treatises in which agriculture is treated as a science—to understand as much of general science as may enable them with less empiricism, and therefore with a greater chance of success, to conduct their trials of manures and composts on their different soils, and to avoid a waste of capital on experiments in draining, irrigation, &c. which are now often conducted contrary to ascertained principles.   A taste for reading itself would assist the diffusion of a knowledge of improvements in agriculture, and would thus increase the intelligence and enterprize of a class of men who contribute so largely to the national wealth.

The clergyman might then rejoice to find his exertions for the erection and support of schools for the children of labourers in the agricultural districts more cordially and steadily seconded by the farmers than they now are.   He would also be able to reclaim from misappropriation educational endowments, on which parochial authorities have for a long time laid their hands; and among the labourers themselves would arise a stronger sense of the value of education to their children. At the present we fear we have for the most part to record, respecting the rural districts, a melancholy void in the means of instruction for the poorer classes.   The exceptions to this rule are attributable almost solely to the interference of the proprietors of the soil, or of the clergy, to whose exertions we must owe any further advance which can at present be made.

But in the towns the influence of the middle class is, from their numbers and intelligence, predominant ; and, consequently, that of the Dissenters is great.   No Government could long exist in this country which should either neglect the legal right which the Established Church has to expect the protection and support of the Executive Government, or which, on the other hand, should refuse to admit that a large body of Her Majesty's subjects who dissent from the Established Church have a legal right to an equal distribution of all the secular advantages derivable from a Government supported by the public funds.

But when to the rights recognized by the law the Dissenters have superadded the claim arising out of the exertions they have spontaneously made to provide for education, in some of the most important districts of this country, we are at a loss to know, on what pretence they can be excluded from sharing the secular benefits of any provision for National Education furnished at the public cost, or how the Government could have been justified, either in formally excluding them from the privilege of educating their teachers in the Normal school, or, (which is equivalent to that), in imposing such religious observances on those teachers, or so inadequately providing for their entire religious freedom, as practically to have occasioned their exclusion.

Nothing would tend so much to increase the political power of religious denominations not agreeing with the Established Church, as to attempt a partial or exclusive distribution of any new civil advantages, after admitting them to a theoretical equality of civil rights. We believe it to be impossible to place on the statute book any such law; but once there, the clamour raised would be so loud and fierce, that any Administration must quail before it, and if Parliament did not listen to the indignant remonstrances of the constituency, this would become the sole topic of electioneering agitation until the new enactment was repealed.

Conceiving the application of the public funds to the exclusive secular advantage of any class of religionists impossible, we are of opinion that two courses only were open to the Committee of Privy Council in proposing the plan of a Normal School.

1. To establish separate Normal Schools for different classes of religionists.

2. To establish a Normal School open to all.

One principle our laws require should be preserved inviolate under all circumstances, viz. that the Established Church should suffer no detriment, but should hold her position among the religious denominations of this country, as the Church, whose head is the Sovereign, and whose institutions are interwoven with those of the temporal power.

If, then, separate Normal Schools were established for different classes of religionists, let us examine in what way an impartial distribution of the secular advantages of such institutions could have been secured. A Normal School being established for the Church, would it be necessary to establish a separate Normal School for each one of the numerous sects, or do those sects admit of some classification into groups for each of which a Normal School might be provided? Clearly the latter is the only practicable plan, and the British and Foreign School Society is founded on a principle which provides schools for the children, and a certain amount of training for the teachers, of the Orthodox Congregational Dissenters and of the Society of Friends. The plan of separate schools for each sect is thus impracticable, and that of a common school for the Orthodox Congregational Dissenters is in practical operation. We may infer, from these premises, that the necessity of distributing impartially the secular advantages of such institutions under the plan of separate Normal Schools for separate classes of religionists would have required at least the following schools : —1. A Normal School for the Church.—2. A Normal School for the Wesleyan Methodists.—3. A Normal School for the Orthodox Congregational Dissenters, and for the Society of Friends.— 4. A Normal School for the Roman Catholics ; and it would have been necessary to make provision for any other classes by admitting them to the secular benefits of one or other of the above schools without imposing any religious observances.

We are content to state, without comment, the scheme which appears to us to afford the only ultimately practicable alternative to the plan proposed by the Government. We do not hesitate to say, the concern of the Committee of Council to preserve the interests of the Church, while they exercised the authority confided to them by the temporal Head of the Church, for the promotion of National Education, so as to protect the rights of conscience, could alone have induced the Committee to prefer the plan which they announced in their minute of the 11th of April.

We have sufficiently vindicated that plan from the charge of a tendency to promote latitudinarianism by our previous remarks —we have now shewn what is evidently the only practicable alternative to the adoption of that plan.

One feature of the recent debates is a source of no little regret to the friends of education. The fact of the want of means of instruction for the people was admitted; but little or nothing transpired indicating that the extent of the void was known.— Had the fearful breadth of this chasm in our National Institutions been perceived, we cannot believe that so much time would have been expended in exaggerating every difficulty obstructing the extension of education to the entire people, whether those difficulties be referable to the religious divisions which unhappily separate the middle classes into hostile camps, or whether they originated in the opposition of any of the existing voluntary associations for primary education. Assuredly the privileges of the Established Church, and also the rights of conscience must be respected, and the religious education of the people is of paramount importance. Neither are we inclined to disparage the value of any of the existing voluntary associations; but it is of infinitely greater importance that the feuds of sects and the interests of bodies incompetent effectually to deal with this national question, should not rob the people of England of the heritage which the Government, after periods of ruinous deprivation, was about to restore to them. The grievance would not be greater if the administration of justice was impeded, or rendered partial, by any attempt to extend spiritual jurisdiction from the Ecclesiastical Courts to the Civil, or to renew the interdicts upon the enjoyment of the civil advantages of society in consequence of some slight to the representative of the Church, or some interference with his spiritual power. But if the whole of this kingdom were placed under an ecclesiastical interdict; if marriages could no longer be solemnized; if the dead were left unburied; and the Churches closed, terrible though the calamity would be, we find a parallel to it in that wide-spread and demoralizing ignorance which paralyzes all the healthful influences of society, if it does not convert its elements into engines of mutual destruction.

APPENDIX.

TABLE, No. I.

District.	Estimated population at period of inquiry.	Children from 3 to 13 estimated, without deducting any from number living between 5 and 15, according to population returns.	Number attending superior private schools, and belonging to middle and upper classes.	Number of children of working classes from 3 to 13, for whom education should be provided, one-third being deducted from the whole number between 3 and 13 for those privately educated, or employed, or sick, or prevented by casualties from attending school, and also deducting the number attending superior private schools.	Number of children of working classes attending endowed and charity schools, and schools attached to public institutions, and infant schools.	Very ill Educated. Number attending dame schools, and common day schools.	Unedu-cated in day schools. Number uneducated in week-day schools.	Total uneducated, and very ill educated.
Manchester	200,000	50,000	2,934	30,400	4,103	11,624	14,641	26,265
Salford	55,000	13,750	882	8,285	1,776	3,357	3,172	6,509
Liverpool	230,000	57,500	4,080	34,254	13,500	11,336	9,418	20,754
Bury	20,000	5,000	174	3,160	652	1,648	860	2,508
York	28,000	7,000	716	3,951	1,926	1,294	731	2,025
	533,000	133,250	8,786	80,050	21,957	29,259	28,822	58,061
Ratio to children of working classes in attendance on school	Ratio to	classes	who	population ought to be	1 in 24	–	–	1 to 9
		–	–	–	1 in 3⅔	–	–	5⅘ to 8
Westminster (in 3 divisions.) St. Martin in Fields, St. Clement Danes, St. Mary-le-Strand, St. Paul's Covent Garden, The Savoy	50,000	10,000	1,017	5,650	1,861	1,124	2,665	3,789
St. John & St. Margaret	54,000	10,800	690	6,510	2,718	1,675	2,117	3,792
St. George, St. James and St. Anne, Soho	111,000	22,000	2,429	12,371	3,382	1,944	7,045	8,989
	215,000	43,000	4,136	24,531	7,961	4,743	11,827	16,570
Ratio to population	–	–	–	1 in 27	–	–	1 to 13
Ratio to children of working classes who ought to be in attendance on school	–	–	1 in 3	–	–	2 to 3

See Reports as to average expense of education in Schools. Lond. & Manchester Statistical Societies.

The table contains the following results for	Manchester, Salford, Liverpool, Bury, York.	Westminster, 3 divisions.
Estimated population at period of inquiry	533,000	215,000
Estimated number of children between 3 and 13	133,250	43,000
Number of children of working classes from 3 to 13, for whom education should be provided	80,050	24,531
Number of children of working classes who attend endowed and charity schools, and schools attached to public institutions and infant schools	21,957	7,961
Number very ill educated in dame and common day schools	29,259	4,743
Number uneducated in week day schools*	28,822	11,827

* Of these several receive some instruction (chiefly religious) in Sunday Schools. See table No. IV.

A Summary of the proficiency of the Prisoners in Norwich Castle, in Reading &c. at the time of their commitment, taken at different periods from 1826 to 1835.

	Could not read at all.	Merely knew the Alphabet.	Could read only so imperfectly as to be of no utility to them.	Could read in the Testament, but could not write.	Could both read and write.	Total of those who could read, and of those who could read and write.	Total uneducated.	TOTAL.
1826 Feb. 7	153	24	40	45	89	134	217	351
Mar. 8	173	28	49	51	99	150	250	400
June 6	223	32	60	56	129	185	315	500
Oct. 24	264	40	68	68	160	228	372	600
Dec. 27	311	43	85	81	180	261	439	700
1827 Mar. 15	350	52	105	91	202	293	507	800
June 13	393	57	119	109	222	331	569	900
Oct. 16	430	60	128	124	258	382	618	1000
1828 Feb. 5	475	66	141	137	281	418	682	1100
April 28	515	67	153	153	312	465	735	1200
Sept. 1	554	72	167	169	338	507	793	1300
Nov. 29	604	77	177	181	361	542	858	1400
1829 Feb. 4	641	81	187	197	394	591	909	1500
April 4	678	88	205	207	422	629	971	1600
July 13	718	94	215	221	452	673	1027	1700
Oct. 21	750	99	228	237	486	723	1077	1800
1830 Jan. 21	793	100	242	253	512	765	1105	1900
Mar. 29	822	105	262	273	538	811	1189	2000
July 28	848	109	286	291	566	857	1243	2100
Nov. 15	875	111	306	310	598	908	1292	2200
Dec. 24	916	117	324	320	623	943	1357	2300
1831 Feb. 10	955	120	339	339	647	986	1414	2400
May 4	989	123	351	357	680	1037	1463	2500
Sept. 3	1019	127	366	378	710	1088	1512	2600
Dec. 7	1052	129	381	395	743	1138	1562	2700
1832 Jan. 31	1084	133	398	415	770	1185	1615	2800
April 9	1113	140	417	433	797	1230	1670	2900
June 25	1146	147	428	445	834	1279	1721	3000
Oct. 15	1175	152	449	461	863	1324	1776	3100
1833 Jan. 5	1204	157	459	479	901	1380	1820	3200
Mar. 19	1238	166	470	494	932	1426	1874	3300
June 18	1268	173	483	511	965	1476	1924	3400
Sept. 27	1296	177	493	533	1001	1534	1966	3500
Nov. 28	1330	186	499	555	1030	1585	2015	3600
1834 Jan. 16	1364	194	508	577	1057	1634	2066	3700
Mar. 22	1397	204	521	599	1079	1678	2122	3800
June 24	1428	211	534	617	1110	1727	2173	3900
Oct. 23	1463	219	540	635	1143	1778	2222	4000
1835 Feb. 10	1499	222	547	651	1181	1832	2268	4100
April 7	1542	231	554	675	1198	1873	2327	4200
July 16	1581	237	561	693	1228	1921	2379	4300
Nov. 4	1611	249	571	715	1254	1969	2431	4400

N.B. All recommittals are omitted, and also those prisoners who may have been committed for too short a time to come under the chaplain's regular and continued instruction.

www.ingramcontent.com/pod-product-compliance
Lightning Source LLC
LaVergne TN
LVHW081347060426

835508LV00017B/1457

9 781535 808897